A
CREED
FOR
A
CHRISTIAN
SKEPTIC

A
CREED
FOR
A
CHRISTIAN
SKEPTIC

MARY MC DERMOTT SHIDELER

There is a great deal of skepticism in
believers; and a good deal of belief in non-
believers; the only question is where
we decide to give our better energy . . . .
"Lord, I believe; help thou mine unbelief"
may, and should, be prayed two ways.

CHARLES WILLIAMS

WILLIAM B. EERDMANS PUBLISHING COMPANY
GRAND RAPIDS, MICHIGAN

To
PROFESSOR ROBERT BRODIE MACLEOD
who trained me
and gave me the courage
to think for myself

CONTENTS

A Note on Theology   9

A Note on the Apostles' Creed   17

PART ONE: THE SELF

1. I   23
2. I believe   25
3. I believe in   36

PART TWO: THE OTHER

4. God   45
5. God the   56
6. God the Father   57
7. God the Father Almighty   62
8. God the Father Almighty, Maker   71
9. God the Father Almighty, Maker of heaven and earth   81

A Note on "Good" and "Love"   86

PART THREE: THE CRUCIAL PROBLEM

10. And in Jesus Christ his only Son, our Lord   93
11. Who was conceived by the Holy Ghost, born of the Virgin Mary   104

12. SUFFERED UNDER PONTIUS PILATE, WAS
    CRUCIFIED, DEAD, AND BURIED   107

13. HE DESCENDED INTO HELL   113

14. THE THIRD DAY HE ROSE AGAIN FROM THE DEAD   116

15. HE ASCENDED INTO HEAVEN   121

16. AND SITTETH ON THE RIGHT HAND OF
    GOD THE FATHER ALMIGHTY   124

17. FROM THENCE HE SHALL COME TO
    JUDGE THE QUICK AND THE DEAD   129

PART FOUR: THE CONSUMMATION

18. I BELIEVE IN THE HOLY GHOST   135

19. THE HOLY CATHOLIC CHURCH, THE
    COMMUNION OF SAINTS   140

20. THE FORGIVENESS OF SINS, THE
    RESURRECTION OF THE BODY   148

21. AND THE LIFE EVERLASTING   156

22. AMEN   158

A NOTE ON SOURCES   163

INDEX   165

A NOTE ON THEOLOGY

MEN AND WOMEN DEVELOP THEOLOGIES WHEN, HAVING FOUND LIFE puzzling to their minds and disturbing to their hearts, they try to work out an understanding of life that will satisfy their intellectual honor and their hearts' needs. The resulting theological structures are likely to differ radically in the way they state the basic issues and in their conclusions, but one imperative set of questions permeates them all: Who am I, and where am I, and what am I doing here? These are universal as well as personal questions, and social as well as individual. Everyone does ask and answer them more or less consciously and more or less adequately. And they are practical as well as theoretical questions. How we answer them will directly or indirectly determine all our actions in and reactions to the world in which we live.

Like other immense and immediate questions, the great theological problems can be broken down into smaller topics that are easier to handle. Western theologians and philosophers traditionally have grouped them under three headings: How do we know what we know, and how can we be certain it is true? (the study of epistemology) ; what kind of a world is this? (metaphysics) ; and what should we be doing? (ethics) .

Every generation is likely to use a different language in discussing these matters, and often the languages differ from one locality to another. The discipline of theology has sometimes acquired a bad reputation because the meaning of its words and concepts was lost when they were transmitted to another context of time or place or situation. A striking example comes from the famous subject for debate in the Middle Ages, "How many angels can stand on the point of a pin?" The issue then at stake is still a lively and important one. To restate it in a way that we find more congenial: "How can something like an idea, which is not made of 'matter', influence something that is 'material', like

9

a brain?" It is one way of asking the philosophers' mind-body problem, and how we answer it will decisively affect our theoretical approach and practical programs in education, medicine, psychotherapy, politics, and a dozen other activities.

For a good many years, such confusions have divided professional theologians from laymen, and the gulf has been deepened by a misconception of another kind. Christian teachers and preachers have spent abundant time in proclaiming the Christian answers to vital human questions, but few of the authorities have made sure at the beginning that their hearers knew what the questions were. They have been like teachers announcing to a class that the correct answer to yesterday's question is 17, without first saying whether it was yesterday's question about the age of Mozart when he wrote *The Magic Flute,* or the number of years in Louis XIV's reign, or the cube root of 4913, or the number of oxygen atoms in a molecule of glucose. An answer without a question is meaningless. With an inappropriate question, an answer will be either wrong or misleading.

Thus it is generally supposed that the statement "God is love" is the Christian answer to the question, "What is the nature of God? What is God like?" Building on this foundation, men have created wonderful and sometimes fearful structures that as they develop seem to reflect less and less of the substance and emphasis of the biblical record. Many scholars now are saying instead that the best and perhaps the only defensible description of the nature of God is found in the Old Testament, where God is reported as having said to Moses, "I AM THAT I AM" — or in a more accurate translation, "I CAUSE TO HAPPEN", I am he who makes things happen. Christians go on from their experience of what happens to say that God loves, creates, judges, redeems, and performs various other functions. In the last analysis, however, only his own "I cause to happen" can be taken as a definitive reply to the question of his own intrinsic nature.

The great questions of theology are familiar to every person who has wondered what life in general, and his own life in particular, are all about. The Christian answers are known at least sketchily to everyone who is acquainted with the rudiments of the Christian faith. But with depressing persistency, we fail to connect the answers with the proper questions, so that we come far short of achieving the liberty and power which have been promised to the followers of Jesus called the Christ.

Still another misunderstanding of theology can be traced to the belief that theological systems present final, unchangeable positions rather than progress reports on a continuing enterprise. Individual theologians, both lay and professional, do indeed reach firm conclusions and enshrine them in systematic forms. But Christian theology is a product of the ongoing Christian community, which simultaneously teaches and is taught by its individual members. Therefore theology is continually in flux. A theologian is Christian not because he surrenders his intellectual integrity to the Christian community or because it officially recognizes him as its spokesman, but because of their mutual confession that they have been called by the same God and so they live from the same roots in history, thought, and worship. They acknowledge the same Father, God in Christ Jesus, and the same Mother, the Church. Thus their disputes are family quarrels, fought out on the familiar terrain of their common heritage.

During some periods of Christian history, theological and ecclesiastical battles have been waged in comparative privacy by people who were well acquainted with the historical, theological, and human background that constitutes the field of Christian discourse. Currently, however, these conflicts have become free-for-alls, involving many whose effort and sometimes agony are largely wasted because they do not know the lie of the land on which the action is occurring, or the nature of the weapons being employed. So they dig trenches to stop helicopters and trust machine guns to protect them from epidemics. Frequently they interpret a plea for understanding as a demand for surrender, or they assume that a new idea is proposed in order to displace an old one, when it may be only an attempt to balance a dangerous overemphasis on the other side. Above all, they tend to hope for a conclusive settlement of claims, when the best that a Christian theology can give them is increasing illumination.

Laymen themselves are responsible in part for their ignorance of Christian history and doctrines, and of the methods

11

of Christian theology. Too often they have clung, in fear or sentimentality or laziness, to the childish forms of the faith that were all they could comprehend when they were children. The churches also bear part of the responsibility. Too often the ecclesiastical shepherds, lay and clerical, have suppressed straightforward teaching of Christianity lest the flocks in their charge find such food unappealing or indigestible. Newborn lambs must have milk — they cannot digest grass — but sheep require pasture to bring them to full growth. The Christian community must provide food for mature men and women as well as for the timid and the young, or else it will sit by, watching hard-pressed adults who need meat, vegetables, and a cup of hot coffee going elsewhere for their dinners. Theologians also are partly responsible. They are prone either to underrate the layman's courage and his capacity for grappling with basic issues, or else to overrate his skill at finding the gist of an elaborate argument. Whatever responsibility remains can be attributed to original sin.

This book was written by a layman for other laymen. It does not concern itself with the questions that theologians are currently asking among themselves or seem to think that laymen ought to ask, but with those being asked by laymen I know. Neither is it an authoritative exegesis of what the Apostles' Creed has meant in the past or ought to mean in the present. Instead, I am using the Creed as the framework for a discussion of the questions and answers that seem to me, as a layman, especially significant for Christian laymen today.

All theology is to some degree confessional, a business of saying, "Here I stand," whether it is the professional theologian confessing that he happens to be more interested in religious empiricism than in the analysis of religious language, or an unschooled layman affirming that he believes even though he does not understand. Inevitably, therefore, much of the time I shall simply be countering one confession with another. In place of "Christianity requires us to believe in certain dogmas and perform certain actions", I shall assert that Christianity calls us to become increasingly responsive — and responsible — to God in Christ Jesus. Instead of showing the Christian life as a state to be achieved, I shall describe it as a continuing process in which the most important thing is not where we are at any particular moment but in what direction we are moving. To me, in this book, it is far less important whether a person has reached the stage where he can believe in the Christian God or any God, than whether he is deeply engaged with the attitudes and experiences and concepts of the world which underlie the traditional Christian doctrines.

Further, all theologians are in some degree anti-something. The theologian is protesting against what he believes to be a serious error or disproportion or omission in other theological statements. My own chief target is the dogmatic spirit — in fundamentalism, liberalism, radicalism, traditionalism, and skepticism itself — that prevents us from thinking lucidly, cogently, and creatively about the Christian faith or our own faiths. Theologians and churches may not intend to stifle thinking, but whatever their intentions, it does happen, and far more widely than is generally supposed. Two of the obstacles to thought must be identified at once. First, the laymen's questions — which often are not clearly articulated — often are not answered on the level of the need that prompted them. As a result, many questioners have become convinced that their inquiries are unanswerable or illegitimate, so they feel guilty even for expressing their difficulties. Second, many of the devout are afraid that the examination of such questions will lead them to lose something represented by their childhood joy at Christmas, their present intuitions of holiness and peace, and their impulse to worship. I have slowly become persuaded that, given these alternatives, it is better for them to live with the contradiction, keeping religion in one compartment of their lives and the rest of their existence in another, than to abandon their loyalty to such profoundly personal, spontaneous responses, or to retreat from the modern world surrounding them.

Here, as I see it, is one of the most fundamental problems for the layman in our time: how he can be intelligent in his faith without subverting his worship, and how he can worship without violating his intellect and his orientation in the world.

It is the problem of integration, of integrity. We are told by persons who are presumably authorities that for "modern" man the concept of a God "out there" is meaningless, and that the classic language concerning God is empty. Knowing ourselves to be "modern" in every other respect, we conclude that our inchoate perceptions of an Other, and our inclination to speak of it in formally exalted language, are shameful. First we are taught to despise our spontaneous insights; then we are elaborately studied to find out why we do not have insight. We are admonished not to worship a divine being because such "other-worldliness" will distract us from our social duties; and when we obey that injunction, we are criticized because we have nothing fresh or healing to contribute to society. The very possibility of integration is denied on every hand and hampered by every means; then we are imperiously told that we are hopelessly fragmented creatures.

If, as many people say, we are living in a post-Christian era, it is not because belief in traditional Christianity is impossible within a scientifically oriented culture, but only because it is prohibited by certain currently fashionable philosophies of science. Now as always, intellectual and imaginative effort is required to perceive the ways of relating current thinking to traditional thought, and the ardent devotion of our ancestors to the passions by which we are stirred. But we are still asking the questions they asked: Who are we? What kind of a world are we living in? Why are we here? Where are we going? How shall we live? When, if ever, shall we reach the fulfilment we crave? Therefore we can be enlightened by the answers our forefathers discerned, even if we do not entirely accept them.

Because I am writing specifically for laymen, my language and approach are not those which are generally used by professional theologians or by ministers. I have taken them principally from lay writers like Charles Williams, C. S. Lewis, and Charles Morgan. Moreover, the following chapters trace only one of the many ways in which the Christian faith can be stated, and neither the form nor the content of my presentation will be approved by all scholars or will satisfy all laymen.

Christianity is a broad river fed by many tributaries and made up of many currents. Hebrew and Greek forms of thinking — to name only two — have contributed richly to its flow. Some beliefs have always been in midstream, such as the importance of the person named Jesus and called the Christ. Others, such as baptism for the dead, have usually been little eddies close to the banks. Yet there is no historical or theological justification for saying that Christianity has no definable boundaries, so that one can believe whatever he pleases and still be in a meaningful sense Christian. Although no single exposition of the faith has ever been universally accepted as definitive, the river can be mapped and we can determine with reasonable assurance whether this or that idea is in the main channel or close to one of the shores, and whether we are travelling along the Christian river or some entirely different stream of thought and action.

Again and again in the history of the Christian community, we have lost the sense of our general direction while we argued over where to sleep for a night. We have sacrificed the vitality of our faith for the sake of precise doctrinal formulations, and checked our movements forward because we were afraid that any slight misstep would result in a permanent disorientation. We have not dared to become like little children because we were afraid of being childish. And in our haste to leap into the future, we have taken short cuts that landed us in deserts or fetid swamps. Hedged about with warnings against excess, we have quenched our enthusiasm long before it was in danger of becoming an obsession, and we have blown out our lanterns because they reminded us that we shall go blind if we stare fixedly at the sun. But while the way of Christian life may be narrow, it is more likely to twist and bend like a river than to run straight like a Roman road, and we who follow it downstream to the sea may be temporarily heading west around one curve while our companions are heading east around another curve, yet both may be travelling in the same current to the same end.

This book does not provide the kind of map which can be

used for navigating shoals. It is offered as an aid in locating the position of the river in relation to the continent of human life through which it flows, and for indicating its course from the biblical sources to the point where we now are in our progress toward the conclusion and fulfilment of our history, and all history, in God.

A NOTE ON THE APOSTLES' CREED

IN PRESENTING THE BASIC CHRISTIAN QUESTIONS AND ANSWERS, I have chosen to follow the structure of the Apostles' Creed because it is a favorite target for critics, and thus has become a test case. As one of my friends commented in a letter to me, "The Apostles' Creed is an admirable example of 'irrational' (some would say 'ridiculous') assumptions. A theology built on this Creed is surely a waste of time at best and completely misleading at worst."

Later conversations with him revealed two salient features in his objection. He was not asking the kinds of questions that the Apostles' Creed was designed to answer; and it had never occurred to him that, in any case, the Christian creeds do not consist of assumptions. On the contrary, they exhibit a pattern of conclusions. They are not digests of information but summaries of wisdom. Consequently, their meaning cannot be received directly even with the help of many explanations, and they become for us living realities only when our own experience confirms and is confirmed by them.

Nobody knows exactly when the Apostles' Creed was written or by whom. There is ample evidence that none of the twelve apostles had anything to do with it, and no evidence even remotely suggesting that they might have written any part of it. Scholarly opinion about its date ranges from roughly 150 to 800 A.D. The clause, "He descended into hell," may have been inserted long after the rest of it was in general use.

Like the other great summaries of Christian doctrine, the Apostles' Creed was compiled so that the Christian faith might be "made known, shared, and protected against misconstructions".[1] Without some official definition, anyone who believed

---

[1] All notes will be found at the rear of the book, on pp. 163-164.

anything — for example, his own deity, the deity of Caesar, or no deity at all — could call himself Christian and present his version of the faith to the uninformed as the one set forth in the New Testament and proclaimed by the corporate church. Any group of persons professing any doctrines could claim to be the authentic Christian church, and shape its teachings, traditions, and institutions into any form they pleased. The Apostles' Creed was written by men who believed it to be an accurate and fair description of Christianity, and it has been accepted as such for centuries by most parts of the church because others agreed with that judgement.

Characteristically, the Christian creeds can be used in either of two ways, which can be compared to the circumference and the center of a circle. In one case, the formula becomes a fence shutting in all who assent to its propositions and shutting out those who doubt or deny them. When someone says, "You cannot be a Christian unless you believe every word of the Apostles' Creed," he is turning it into an enclosure, a high, rigid, and divisive wall. The alternative is to take the Creed as the center of concentric circles which may be large or small in the beginning, but may contract or expand as they develop. In this case, detailed conformity is not the critical consideration, but direction of reference. What matters is whether one continually refers his own thinking to the center, testing his experience against that standard and testing the standard by his experience. He is then free to question, to examine, to explore, to wait, and to grow, as well as to hear creatively those who have received a word or a grace different from his own. The use of the Creed as a center rather than a wall permits and even requires the Christian to be distinguished from those who refer their lives to some other center. At the same time, it establishes him in an abiding relationship with all who have taken as their center of reference the Christian faith and community.

We do not and cannot know precisely what the author or authors of the Apostles' Creed intended by the words and phrases they used, any more than we can know what Shakespeare's inner thoughts may have been when he wrote his tragedies. All we know is what they said, which may not be exactly what they wanted to say, or quite as unambiguous as they presumably hoped it was. For example, the Apostles' Creed begins with the word "I", rather than the "We" which many modern creeds employ, and we cannot be sure what determined their choice. It may have been because "I" was then customary, or for some weightier reason like the one I suggest in my first chapter. There and elsewhere I may be forcing the evidence; or I may be ignoring evidence; and nowhere have I tried to cover all the possible interpretations, or to trace how contemporary thought developed from its biblical and traditional sources. The Apostles' Creed as we have it was derived from a number of earlier formulas in other languages, but it is the English translation commonly used in Protestant worship which baffles and infuriates and illuminates the laymen who, like me, are less interested in what it once said to others than in whether it can possibly say anything to us today.

It has been repeatedly proposed that congregations should discontinue the practice of using the Apostles' Creed in their services of worship because it is not self-evidently clear. I disagree, because some statement of faith is needed, and any creed which is brief enough to be used at all will need interpretation. A creed is not a primer for the uninformed, but a concise summary of a complex body of experience, and the new creeds recently adopted are also unintelligible unless they are given the same kind of study that is needed for understanding the traditional creeds. Moreover, by retaining the Apostles' Creed we hold firmly onto our past; we remind ourselves that we have a history; we exhibit to the world our continuity with our forebears. The ancient creeds prevent us from becoming theologically and culturally parochial. Repeating them, we gain strength for resisting our natural tendency to deify our local and temporary preoccupations. We do well to formulate and study new creeds. We do not do well to refuse the traditional creeds an equivalent degree of careful and intelligent attention.

The Apostles' Creed has neither the poetry of the so-called Athanasian Creed, nor the precision of the Nicene. Its particular virtues are its utter simplicity — every word is necessary and no necessary idea is omitted — and the logic of its structure.

Its first phrase, "I believe in," refers to the Self. The second group of phrases defines the Other whom the Self confronts. The third and longest section, on Jesus the Christ, describes the ways in which Self and Other interact. The final paragraph deals with the purpose and consummation of that interaction. Taken as a whole, its pattern is magnificently coherent, every proposition growing out of and into every other, so that together they form a fabric that is tightly woven and exquisitely designed.

PART ONE:
THE SELF

I believe in

Chapter 1

I

THE FIRST WORD OF THE APOSTLES' CREED ANSWERS THE QUESTION, "Who's talking?" It pinpoints responsibility. To say "We" would leave the way open for us to slip by with the mental reservation, "Oh yes, on the whole most Christians do believe these statements. I want to be a member of the Christian community, and I do not want to arouse controversy or lose my friends. Therefore I shall recite the whole thing even though I do not really believe it." A declaration that "we" make has the nature of a party platform: nobody objects very seriously if individually we subscribe to some items and reject others. But everybody's responsibility becomes, in practice, nobody's responsibility, and the "I" pins us down.

Most of us detest being pinned down. It is one of our most deeply rooted objections to being Christian. Definite statements tend to have definite implications which, if we are honest, compel us to definite action, and we heartily dislike compulsion even from within. Further, we cannot foretell when we take any stand what all its consequences will be, but we know from experience that very likely some of them will be disagreeable. It is easier and safer to be an observer, comfortably free from responsibility, than to participate fully with all the risks and duties that full participation entails.

At times, of course, any participant must stand aside from what he is doing to observe it and himself with all the detachment he can muster, so that afterwards he can re-enter the situation more wisely and profoundly. Then his disengagement becomes the means to intensify his participation, rather than a way to avoid it. Much too often, however, detachment expresses a refusal to become personally involved, and the "I" of the Creed proclaims that the Christian involves himself responsibly in what follows.

Contemporary writers of creeds sometimes use "we" as a way of emphasizing the authenticity and power of the Christian community in a society where loneliness and alienation are epidemic. There is much merit in this approach. We become selves in the first place by our interaction with other selves, and Christians by contact with other Christians: in human development, society precedes individuality. But the "we" of the Christian community is created as each "I" says "we". Its bond of union is produced by a multitude of concurring commitments. In the Apostles' Creed, the concept of community is introduced later. The formula starts with the irreducible one who has been nurtured by society until he has attained individuality, and now is ready to determine for himself what responsibilities he shall undertake.

Chapter 2

I BELIEVE

AT EVERY STEP IN THE STUDY OF THEOLOGY, AS WELL AS IN MOST other affairs of life, we come across questions like: How do you know that? Are you certain? Can you prove it? Where did you get that idea? The authorities disagree — how can you tell which is right? What are the facts? Where is your evidence? The Apostles' Creed begins its answer to these questions with "I believe", not "I know" or "It is true" or simply "God is", and the choice of verb is a fortunate one for us. It releases us from the impossible task of proving that the statements in the Creed, and our Christian beliefs, are absolutely, ultimately, and irrefutably true.

In this respect, Christianity is no better off — and no worse — than any other field of knowledge or inquiry, because so far as scholars have yet been able to determine, there is nothing which man knows or can know without any possibility of alteration or extension or refutation. That sounds extreme, but the statement is based on meticulous study of the ways by which man learns and thinks, ways which are usually grouped under four headings: sense experience, reason, authority, and revelation.

Sense experience includes everything that comes to us by means of our sensory nervous system. Through the receptors for sight, hearing, touch, temperature, position, and all the others, we become acquainted with the world around us, with our own bodies, and possibly with our selves. By and large we can safely trust our senses but they contradict themselves and each other frequently enough that we cannot rely on them completely. Our lives may actually be what we sometimes wish they were, only dreams, although generally we take for granted that the world exists approximately as it appears to be, and

ourselves in it. What we normally do is to presuppose a reasonably exact connection between what we perceive and what we
believe is actually there: that because the cloud looks red to
us, it is red; that because we feel ground under our feet, it is
there; that because we think, we exist. But presuppositions are
not proofs, and these presuppositions cannot be proved by any
method known to philosophy, the sciences, theology, or any
other discipline.

Reason can give us final certainty, but only of one particular
and limited kind. For example, it can be conclusively demonstrated that two triangles which are congruent with a third
will be congruent with each other, but that can be proved, in
the full meaning of "proof", only if a number of other things
are presupposed: the rules of logic and geometry, a frame of
reference for the argument, and so on. In mathematics and
logic, which represent the purest forms of reason, a set of definitions and acceptable procedures is laid down, but the existence
of objective referents for those definitions and procedures cannot be proved, and the mathematician and logician make no
attempt to prove them. They do not presuppose that there
exist, anywhere, entities corresponding to their categories and
symbols, such as actual triangles. They work within a frame
of reference that they have deliberately created for their own
purposes, and their proofs remain absolutely valid only within
that framework. Thus reason can provide ultimate, positive
certainty only on the basis of its underlying presuppositions
and principles. It cannot prove that the presuppositions or principles themselves are true.

Authorities can be divided into two kinds. First there are the
testimonies of persons who report to us on conditions existing
beyond our own experience: letters from friends, communications from experts, books written long ago. Without them, our
lives are bounded by a nutshell. But we receive their contri-
butions through our fallible senses and interpret them with our
fallible minds, and those whose word we accept as authoritative
have depended upon their sensory apparatus and reasoning,
which may be no more dependable than our own. Moreover,
when we want advice from a specialist on anything from auto-

mobile repair to theological doctrines, it is we who must decide whom to take as our final authority, and what basis we shall employ for choosing among conflicting authorities. We cannot rely unconditionally upon anyone else for the same reasons that we cannot rely unconditionally upon ourselves.

Second, we are subject to experiences that produce in us such emotions of utter certainty that we are compelled to believe in their validity. For instance, few of us can seriously doubt the real existence of a world outside ourselves. It so emphatically resists and supports us that our very identity as persons depends upon our accepting its reality. We could not reject our belief in it without jeopardizing our most intimate stability and continuity. To take another instance, certain persons and ideas do command our obedience; and our submission to them, whether willing or unwilling, demonstrates their authority over us. Out of this sort of overwhelming conviction have come Thomas the Doubter's "My Lord and my God", Martin Luther's "Here I stand", and the vows of innumerable lovers. Even so, that an experience has this effect does not make it an infallible guide to truth. The force of its impact does not guarantee its accuracy or ensure the adequacy of the conclusions we draw from it. The strongest emotional assurance cannot give us immunity to intellectual error.

Some of the insights and events which carry this kind of authority are classified by certain scholars as revelations, a word that I avoid as much as possible because it can mean two things that are almost universally confused. One is the impression that something is revealed. The other is the description or interpretation we place upon it. Thus we see a cloud having a specific color: that is the experience, the encounter. Then we employ words or paint to capture its exact hue, saturation, and brilliance: that is the interpretation. Or we suddenly seem to grasp the complete meaning of everything in God: we receive a "divine revelation". Then we try to state its meaning in whatever concepts we happen to be familiar with: the interpretation. In reverse, a stranger is described to us: the interpretation. Later we meet him and recognize him from the description: the encounter. Some theologians, and most laymen, include in "revelation" both the encounter and the interpretation. Others limit the word to the event of the encounter. The narrower definition is much more satisfactory, because to combine the two activities under the one word leaves us unsure of what we are talking about. It must be noted, however, that all thought about such experiences, and all communications regarding them, necessarily require interpretation.

Nothing in this analysis prevents us from believing that some so-called divine revelations are from God, or that all of them are. But even if we are correct in believing them to have a divine source, we must never forget that a finite mind cannot comprehend an infinite reality, and that inevitably our interpretations are conditioned by what we had believed and experienced before the event occurred. Since revelations must be trimmed down in order to enter our finite and fallible minds, and since our minds impose their own structures and processes upon the encounters, the claim that revelations give absolute, ultimate, and irrefutable truth cannot be sustained.

All the principal ways of knowing — sense experience, reason, authority, and revelation — are reasonably dependable. None is absolutely dependable, and no combination of them can give us unqualified assurance of completely accurate and certain knowledge. The theologian cannot prove incontestably that any God exists. The physicist cannot fully prove that the principles of thermodynamics are true, or the biologist that evolution occurred, or the historian that any past event actually happened, or anyone that there is a ground beneath him. Each of these persons finally must rest his case upon the decision to trust his senses, his reasoning processes, the testimony of others, and various of his notably impressive encounters. Speaking precisely, he does not know: he believes.

Yet faced with the impossibility of absolute proof about anything, we walk across the floor as if we were indeed absolutely, ultimately, and irrefutably certain of its reality and its capacity to bear our weight. And why should we not believe it? The floor consistently appears to be there; it faithfully holds us up; and nothing in others' experience contradicts our experience of it. So why not take as fact that it is in reality what it seems to be? What is gained by being skeptical about it? We need to be aware that our presuppositions are not facts because we are continually bombarded with "proofs" for this, that, and the other, and unless we understand the bases for such arguments, we are likely to be deceived by them. All through history, the counterclaims have been flung back and forth, "It can be proved that God exists" and "It can be proved that God does not exist". In both cases, when the proofs are pushed far enough, it will be found that they are resting upon presuppositions and not upon factual evidence. Both protagonists are assuming that our ideas about things are accurate representations of the things themselves, or that logical inferences produce indubitable certainty without regard to the premises from which the logician is operating, or that one set of experiences is somehow more valid or significant than another, or something. In actuality, however, neither statement about the existence of God can be proved beyond the shadow of doubt to be either true or false.

What we believe about our capacity for observing and knowing will directly affect our response to every idea and person and situation that we meet. If we believe that we possess already, or have access to, the full and final truth about something or everything, we shall ultimately — if not immediately — cease to observe and wonder and learn. We shall starve our minds and then our hearts. On the other hand, if we believe that being human, we are finite and thus always to some degree inadequate in our thinking and perceiving, there is at least a fair chance that we shall continue our search for further evidence and more penetrating vision, and will pay attention to information and experience that correct or amplify our beliefs.

Another reason for being precise about the limits of human knowledge is that vague beliefs produce muddled behavior, inconsistent beliefs lead to inconsistent behavior, and erroneous beliefs result in all sorts of blunders and oversights. For how many years was Europe's discovery of the New World delayed by the conviction that the earth is flat? How many persons have tightly closed their minds to Christianity because they

29

were once taught a superficial or corrupted version of it? How often have we struggled to make ourselves feel loving because we did not know that love as Jesus taught it is not a feeling of affection but an attitude of the will?

The Creed's "I believe" is consistent with our limitations as finite beings. We are not gods. We are men, and it is always possible that a man may be wrong in believing whatever he does believe. The honest and intelligent believer necessarily has a skeptical strain in him, a niggling little doubt or a great nagging one. It is both reasonable and practical, however, to assume that our senses give us approximately accurate information about the world, that the canons of sound reasoning should usually be obeyed, and that what we learn from others can for the most part be trusted. Although the evidence for the dependability of the floor is not conclusive, it is sufficient for most of our purposes, like the evidence for the principles of thermodynamics, biological evolution, and the reality of the past. Our observations and rationality agree on them, and our fellows report that they perceive, think, and believe along closely similar lines. Thus Christianity takes its preliminary stand on a ground that is necessary for day-to-day living and defensible for theoretical inquiry: a skepticism about knowledge which is based on the recognition of man's finitude, which is compatible with his confidence that he is capable of learning almost indefinitely, and which frees him from the arrogance that would otherwise petrify his intellect, imagination, and behavior.

Once we have recovered from the shock — and often it is a shock — of realizing that we cannot have absolute certainty in any of our mental operations, we shall find it not as uncomfortable or insecure a position as we may have expected. While "an extremely high degree of probability" may not generate as pleasant an emotional state as "absolutely proved", it is a far more adequate principle upon which to live and, as will become evident a little later, it carries some implications that more than make up for its relatively minor deficiency.

But a major problem remains. In order to think at all, we must presuppose something, if only as simple an axiom as "Some things are more important than others". Without some such ground for thought, we should remain forever on a dead center. We could not determine if any idea were significant or trivial, because we should have no standard by which to measure it and could create no framework in which it might find a place. We could not discover if a chain of reasoning were consecutive or broken, because all connections among ideas would be arbitrary. We could not detach our attention from one thing in order to concentrate upon another except on the basis of chance or impulse, because all things would be equally important — or unimportant — to us. As we cannot walk unless we have ground under our feet to support us, so we cannot think without a supporting structure of presuppositions.

For the most part, we acquire our key presuppositions unconsciously in the process of growing up. From our birth we are encircled by societies based on unspoken agreements which are all the more strictly enforced for being unexamined and which usually are not recognized as the ground for the common life of their members. Since our parents and teachers take for granted that some things are more important than others, and our natural inclinations reinforce that belief, we rarely question it or notice that it is precisely an axiom, an assumption, an article of belief. Once we see it for what it is, however, we must do something about it, and only two possibilities are open to us on issues like this one. Either we accept the thesis that some things are more important than others, or we reject it. There is no middle ground between these extremes, no matter how "important" is defined or who defines it. It is not a "both-and" but an "either-or" proposition, and we must take a stand on it. We must choose.

The choice is forced upon us by the nature of action. As I fashion an illustration, I am not sure that it says exactly what I mean. For a considerable time — through several drafts of the paragraph, perhaps through galley proofs — I can delay the decision between keeping it and throwing it away, or I can revise it more or less radically. But at some stage I shall have to do one or the other. I cannot do both, and I cannot do neither. Nor can I evade the problem by filing it away for use in some other project. That would still mean discarding it from

31

this one. Yes, or no? An agnostic can waver for a lifetime between belief and disbelief in God, but every action he performs will reflect one or the other. Whatever his degree of intellectual commitment or detachment, he cannot temporize so as to act on the basis of "maybe or maybe not", any more than he can act as if the contradictory propositions "all things are equally important" and "some things are more important than others" are simultaneously true. He can jump back and forth from one to the other; he cannot stop in the middle. If there are a thousand possibilities before him, he still can act on only one, which means that he must refuse all the remaining options. Even a withdrawal into catalepsy cannot save him from the necessity of choosing, because such a retreat in itself reflects an implicit choice. The nature of action inexorably demands a commitment to something.

Unfortunately, we do not have access to any neutral ground from which we can view and judge the alternatives objectively. No position can be evaluated except from the vantage point of another position. While we can and sometimes must change our basic assumptions, if we do so very radically and very often, we shall see as little of the world as a passenger in a stunting plane and likely will become as sick. In the end, all we can do is to choose what we shall believe, which places upon us a grave responsibility. Beliefs — not only in religion, but in all fields — come in many shapes, sizes, colors, and materials, and clearly some beliefs will represent reality more adequately than others.

One of our most useful guides here is coherence: how strongly and delicately our presuppositions and the different pieces of our information and experience can be fitted together to form a unified pattern, without contradictions, without twisting any items out of shape, and without the need for inventing a hypothetical principle (such as a "life force") to serve as a bond of union. For instance, the belief that man evolved from a one-celled organism is not coherent with the belief that God created man directly out of the dust by an act of special creation, and any theology that tries to affirm both at once will not be coherent. In the strict sense, it will be incoherent. There are several ways by which the doctrines of evolution and special creation can be modified in the attempt to make them coherent with one another, and scholars have had absorbing and spirited arguments on the merits of these proposals. So far, however, no solution has been generally accepted.

A second guide is inclusiveness. A pattern of beliefs can cohere admirably, but leave out of consideration ideas or types of experience that are widely held to be important. They may be disregarded, of course, because the believer considers them to be unimportant. But on the whole, a theology which brings together coherently an extensive range of facts, perceptions, and modes of thought may properly be valued above one that is restricted to a narrower range.

Some theologians fail in inclusiveness because they ignore the findings of science about the world. Others omit everything not attested by science, such as human love or the apprehensions of beauty and goodness. Still others quietly eliminate anything outside their private experiences: they delete the witness of the historical church or of non-Christian religions, or of persons with other temperaments or training. Often the little theologies are wonderfully coherent, but their makers achieve that virtue by committing intellectual sins of omission. The great theologians, however, try to include the entire wealth of human life, everything that man has observed or reasoned or felt, and to bring it all into their structure of understanding. Necessarily they fail to attain perfect inclusiveness: they are human and therefore finite, but their intention is serious and honest.

Coherence and inclusiveness do not provide an adequate basis for choosing among presuppositions because after these specifications have been met, too many alternatives remain. A third standard is more deeply personal and more difficult to define; the two best names for it that I know are "beauty" and "elegance". The structure exhibits proportion, balance, simplicity, grace, appropriateness, order, in a way that delights the mind and exalts the heart. It satisfies as great art or an exquisitely organized mathematical demonstration does, even if we cannot explain how or why it is satisfying.

For some persons, a fourth standard is as important as all the others combined. Patterns of thought affect action: what kind of action results from putting a belief into practice? What ethic grows out of it? What sort of life does it produce? If one were to follow it consistently, would he have to isolate himself from his fellows, or treat persons as if they were things, or kill those who disagreed with him? Can the principle be practised consistently at all, or does it give rise to mutually contradictory demands upon the believer? A related question cannot be avoided, but is of dubious value as evidence: do we respect the persons who already adhere to the belief? Here we must be extremely cautious, because persons often profess one doctrine but live by another that may be "better" or "worse" than what they say or consciously think. They can act against their declared principles, revealing that they are divided beings — and most of us do and most of us are. So if persons who claim to be Christians behave no better than self-professed non-Christians, three questions have to be answered before Christianity can be written off as unproductive or irrelevant. Do such persons hold the Christian faith as it has traditionally been defined by those who have studied its history, or do they apply the name to a position that has historically been rejected by informed Christians? Are such persons diligent, intelligent, and imaginative in their effort to practise Christianity? And might their behavior be still more objectionable if they adhered to some other belief? Only after answering those questions can we decide whether Christianity should be judged by their lives.

It does not necessarily follow that a theology which is coherent, inclusive, elegant, and has admirable consequences for living will be true, in the sense of accurately reflecting the nature of things as they are. But if, as we continually and legitimately presuppose, our minds and lives are part of the reality we are investigating, then a theology that satisfies our minds and ennobles our lives will presumably be closer to the truth than a chaotic, narrow, and disproportioned theology that offends our intelligence and debases our lives.

When the informed Christian says "I believe", he is stating that his conclusions are based upon presuppositions, that presuppositions are necessary for thought, and that they cannot be proved. He is announcing that he has chosen this one set of presuppositions from among the many alternatives available to him. He is convinced that they are true and is loyal to them, but he knows that he does not know — absolutely, ultimately, and irrefutably. In essence, with these two words he declares that he is human.

In what follows, I shall use the words "know" and "knowledge" in their usual sense, as meaning "Given these presuppositions, it follows —" or "The evidence clearly indicates —" or "We have become convinced —", on the assumption that we are using our senses, reason, and authoritative source materials with a judicious recognition of their limitations. The convenience of ordinary language here outweighs its dangers. When I mean "absolute, ultimate, and irrefutable knowledge", I shall say so.

Chapter 3

I BELIEVE IN

"I BELIEVE" INDICATES INTELLECTUAL ASSENT TO AN IDEA OR AGREE-ment with a person. I believe the chemist when he says that water is made of hydrogen and oxygen. I believe that some things are more important than others. I do not believe that the floor will cave in on me without warning. This is sometimes called "formal belief", to distinguish it from "belief in" or "faith", which includes two other kinds or degrees of belief: real, and unitive.

Unitive belief is fairly rare, and needs to be mentioned here primarily in order to caution the unwary that it can happen to anyone. It is not in any way essential for Christian faith, either as a prerequisite or as a consummation. The best descrip-tion of it that I know of comes from St. Paul: "I live, yet not I, but Christ liveth in me." Something takes hold of one's life like the onrush of a tide so that he no longer acts from his own power but action takes place through him. According to the accounts we have of that state, which are principally from the contemplative and mystical traditions, the person who receives unitive belief can interpret the event as significant or trivial; either way, he can isolate it from his theology and his daily life or incorporate it into them. But he cannot reach unitive belief by his own efforts any more than he can compel himself to become a genius in music or languages, and he cannot by his own will control the times of its coming and going. We are responsible for our formal and real beliefs, for the ways we think and for what we trust. We are not responsi-ble for having or not having unitive belief. It is a gift which may be bestowed upon those whom we would consider unde-serving, and withheld from those who appear worthy of it.

Formal belief — intellectual conviction — becomes real belief or faith at the point where we act upon it. When, after considering evidence for and against the proposition that so-and-so is true, we come to a definite conclusion, we have reached formal belief. When our conclusion influences our further thinking and behavior, we have faith. We not only believe it; we believe in it. We trust it enough that we allow it to determine how we live. Real belief is demonstrated in a small but significant way every time we walk across a floor without thinking about what we are doing. We should behave differently if we really believed that what appeared to be a solid floor actually consisted of painted paper laid across an abyss. The Christian, having real belief in a loving God, behaves differently from the person who really believes all notions of God to be convenient but rather juvenile projections of men's current emotional states. We can have formal belief without real belief: I believe that the big dog down the street is friendly, but when he rushes toward me I am afraid. And we can have faith without intellectual assent: a convinced atheist may, in a crisis, find himself praying to a God.

As we cannot think without presupposing something, we cannot act without believing in something, without having faith. Indeed, the connection is so close that "to presuppose" can be defined as having faith in an idea, and "having faith" can be defined as a form of presupposing. In both cases, the decisive requirement is not knowledge or insight or a warm feeling of security, but courage, and the extreme opposite of faith is not disbelief or uncertainty or skepticism, but fear. It is a contrast which Jesus himself set forth: "Why are you fearful? Have you not yet faith?"

We may be afraid of being hurt or of being wrong, of death or of life. Our fear may be a momentary or a permanent state, excited by many things or by one thing only — like spiders. But whatever its occasion, duration, or magnitude, fear in some degree paralyzes our ability to act or think. Our muscles freeze or our minds congeal. This is very different from the prudent wisdom that leads us to evaluate alternatives and then to follow steadily and humbly the best we know. It is also different from the serene acceptance of human limitations. I am speaking now of that fear and fearfulness in which we dare not move intellectually or physically because we dare not trust anything, and for the same reason we dare not stay where we are.

Such fear is entirely reasonable. Our friends may turn against us at any moment. The floor may give way at our next step. The universe may reveal itself to be a fraud or a hallucination. We can have no absolute assurance that anything is actually dependable enough that we are safe in trusting it, and we have no methods by which we can infallibly determine whether it is. Depth beyond depth this takes us, like Dante through hell to the center of the world. Yet our path, like his, leads out again to the day. If we are courageous and persistent enough in our skepticism, we shall come to doubt not only our beliefs but also our doubts. It cannot be conclusively proved that something — anything — is absolutely trustworthy? Neither can its untrustworthiness be conclusively proved. Our friends may remain unswervingly loyal. The floor may always hold us up. Our suspicions of the universe may be entirely unjustified.

At the point where we become skeptical of our very skepticism, we must decide which set of doubts we prefer to live with: the partial skepticism of the fearful, or the wholehearted skepticism of the faithful. The alternative is to swing abjectly back and forth, miserably trying to evade the decision, and miserably failing because evasion is in fact a choice for cynicism and fear.

In ordinary speech, we frequently use the word "skeptical" as if it meant cynical or suspicious or incredulous, just as we often use the word "philosophical" as if it meant stoical. Certainly doubt can lead to denial, although it can equally well lead to affirmation and trust, but this is peripheral. What is central to the skeptic is not belief in this or that idea, but opposition to the dogmatic spirit of pride that leads men to claim for human beings a superhuman and inhuman authority. Thus when the greatest of the philosophical skeptics, David Hume, demonstrated our inability to prove finally and conclusively that one event actually causes another, he did not destroy the principle of causality as such. What he did was to achieve a stunning victory over the intellectual arrogance which asserts that it is possible for a finite creature to prove it. Similarly, to be skeptical about Christianity is not to renounce the faith, but to insist for ourselves and others on the imperative need for humility. As skeptics, we can have unconditional faith, but we cannot have unconditional knowledge.

The Christian skeptic can be both Christian and skeptical because he knows that in accepting the Christian faith, he is trusting uncertainties. He cannot live at all without believing in something; he has chosen to believe in this. Probably his choice will be determined in part by what he conceives to be the coherence, inclusiveness, and elegance of its intellectual structure, in part by its consequences for living, and in part by still other factors less easy to identify. He will likely be aware that in some degree his choice reflects an indefinable personal preference. Once made, however, the decision places his feet on a ground as stable as the floor beneath him. For most purposes he will not call his new presuppositions into question any more seriously than he does the impermeability of the floor, or more often than the scientist questions the validity of the scientific enterprise — which is also built upon presuppositions that the scientist has chosen to believe in. The Christian skeptic, having decided to trust the Christian presuppositions, proceeds really to trust them.

No doubt he will have moments or hours or years of wondering if his choice were the right one. Such periods are liable to descend upon all who are not incurably fanatic, with respect not only to religion, but also to marriage, vocations, and every other commitment. During such times, the Christian skeptic is consoled and strengthened by his awareness that the choice between Yes and No is never between an utterly secure position and various doubtful ones, but among a number of positions all of which are precarious. He is not obsessed by the futile dream of inhabiting a fortress impregnable to uncertainty, anxiety, and error.

Some theologians, even today, maintain that faith begins where reason leaves off, and so teach that the Christian's duty is meekly to accept the doctrines of the faith without questioning them. They hold that while it may be legitimate to ask what a doctrine means, such inquiry is not necessary and may be dangerous. Others, including many of the greatest figures in Christian history, have declared that the Christian is under obligation to use all the intelligence he has in examining what these ideas mean, in testing their validity, and in exploring their sources and implications. To them, the faith is not a magical formula to be parroted, but a vision of the world to be comprehended. Only a few are called to the intensive study by which theologians are formed in their vocation. All men, however, are responsible for what they trust and do not trust, and therefore no Christian can be exempt from the responsibility for learning as much as he can, and for doubting as extensively as he must.

At times, certainly, our faith can properly outstrip our comprehension. Having conscientiously worked our way through the doctrine of the fatherhood of God and having decided to believe in it, we may deliberately go on to believe in other Christian doctrines that we have not yet been able to clarify for ourselves. In the same way, when we have learned to respect the authority of a friend in a particular area, we are likely to accept his authority in that field even when he is speaking beyond our depth. If in time we achieve a competence equal to his, we may reject his judgement. Meanwhile, since we have more reason to question our own qualifications than his, at least we do not dismiss his considered opinion out of hand. The position, "I do not understand, but for the time being I shall take your word for it because I have found that your word was good in other matters," is entirely compatible with Christian skepticism, so long as the believer is honest with himself on what he is doing, and selects his authority with as much care as he employs in choosing his intellectual presuppositions and the articles of his faith. We do in fact have formal and real belief in persons as well as in ideas, and the same balance of faith and doubt is, or should be, present in our relationship to both.

"I believe in": the Apostles' Creed does not require that all questions should be answered, all doubts smothered, all fears quenched. Rather, it calls for faith which is responsible and intelligent, and for courageous action on the basis of what we have responsibly, intelligently, and courageously decided to believe.

PART TWO:
THE OTHER

God the Father Almighty,
Maker of heaven and earth

Chapter 4

GOD

THE FIRST THREE WORDS OF THE APOSTLES' CREED DESIGNATE WHO is doing what: I believe in. The next word, God, carries a heavier freight in our day than at many earlier times because of a question that has become prominent only within recent years. Its most sensational expression is found in the works of Bonhoeffer, Sartre, and the death-of-God theologians: Is there any Other, natural or supernatural, in which man can safely trust as the support or reference for his whole life? Or must he ultimately depend upon himself in his essential being, either as an individual person or as a representative of that splendid abstraction, Humanity?

The traditional Christian answer has been that the object of the Christian's faith is a being who is radically distinct from man and humanity. Whether that Other is most appropriately described as being "up there" or "out there", or perhaps "down there" as the ground of being, it is at least *there* and not *here*. We discover it not by looking inward at ourselves but by looking outward, either beyond "me" or "us", or by using "me" and "us" as lenses to look through. Against this, a number of contemporary theologians are saying that if we do look beyond ourselves, we see nothing at all, and that if we try to look through ourselves, we find that the lens is opaque. Philosophers have analyzed the historical name for that Other, God, and have demonstrated that the concept is logically incoherent and has no explicit reference that their philosophy can define or defend. Social historians have demonstrated that belief in a god has repeatedly had pernicious results for societies and individuals. And artists, journalists, and other commentators on the modern scene have vehemently denounced all talk of any god as irrelevant to "modern" man.

The strongest consideration which the Christian skeptic can offer in reply to these allegations is his conviction, drawn primarily not from philosophical argument but from living experience, that he has in fact been met by an Other who deserves the name God. If he cannot go so far, he can at least offer his confidence, based on his trust in other persons, that there does exist such an Other even though he has not yet encountered it directly. How he has reached his conclusion will depend upon biographical details that differ as widely as biographies do. The form in which the Other appears, if at all, will also vary. It may assert itself as an implacable moral demand, an intellectual imperative, a sense of an all-encompassing unity, a perception of the holy, an apprehension of a divine being. The effect is that the person submits unconditionally to something that is unconditionally outside himself, not from expediency or in expectation of a reward, but because he must: when it confronts him, its glory sends him to his knees.

This kind of Other can no more be encountered by dispassionate study than colors or sounds are encountered by reading books about them. Intellectual deliberations can clear away misconceptions that would prevent us from meeting or recognizing it, but the intellect is only one of the functions of persons, and it is persons who respond when they come in contact with the ultimately Other, whether it be conceived of as a thing like a law or a force, or as a divine person.

Christianity is not and has never been primarily a philosophical or theological system that appeals to men principally because of its coherent rational structure. If it were, those who happen not to be intellectually gifted or who lack educational advantages would have small chance of becoming fully Christian, and mental agility or profundity would be, in effect, a special passport to sanctity. On the contrary, Christianity has always pertained to the whole person and calls for response from his whole being. Therefore it is open equally to the worldly-wise and the simple, the ignorant and the erudite, the dull and the swift of mind. The intellect must not be wronged, because what the reason rejects, the heart cannot for long embrace except at the price of a breach in integrity. But intellectual assent cannot substitute for personal faith, formal for real belief.

At this point it becomes necessary to consider what is meant by the concept "person", in the sense not of distinctive personality, but of the difference between personal beings and impersonal things. The distinction is extraordinarily difficult to put into words, although in day-by-day living we usually make it without perplexity or conscious effort, whether we limit "persons" to members of our immediate families and behave toward all other human and non-human beings as "things", or whether we include under "person" a pet animal, the computers that are spoken of as mechanical brains, and the ships that are always referred to as "she". In examining the reasons underlying our choice among such words, it becomes evident that a being develops personhood only through contact with other persons. It is an acquired characteristic, transmitted by direct derivation. A human infant who is treated as a case but not as a person will not grow properly in mind or body. An adult who is consistently treated as a thing can lose his capacity for personal response and become to all intents and purposes a thing — a fact attested by numerous reports from concentration camps and institutions for the care of the mentally disturbed. An animal in close association with persons who behave personally toward it may develop "personality" in a way that a wild animal does not. We are persons because we have been dealt with personally.

In practice, it appears that we do not differentiate between persons and things on the ground that persons are less reliable and more complex than things, or self-evidently higher in the scheme of existence, but instead on the kind of demand that they place upon us and the kind of response we choose to make in our relationships with them. Thus we obscurely sense that we can deal adequately with sticks and stones without bringing into play the depths of our selves that must be engaged if we are to have satisfactory relationships with our husbands or wives or children or friends. The very nature of the world invites us to distinguish between persons and things, although it does

47

not compel us to or determine for us where we shall draw the line.

The traditional Christian concept of a personal God arises directly out of what many persons have discovered when they struggled with the anguish and exultation, the routines and accidents of their lives: that in those events, an absolute personal demand was laid upon them. They were met by an Other who evoked an infinitely deeper and more intense response than any natural or human agency could call forth. So when the Christian says, "I believe that the ultimate reality is personal, that God is a person," one of the things he can mean is that he finds it inappropriate or inadequate or degrading to respond impersonally in the encounter with that Other. He cannot treat it as a thing without violating his own reality as a person. But here, as in all other circumstances where we distinguish persons from things, we finally do not determine by neutral observation who or what is, in its essence, a person, because there is no neutral ground from which we can observe the situation. We choose whom or what we shall treat personally, both when we initiate an approach and when we respond to another's initiative.

How can we be certain that the ultimate Other whom we have met, or whom others declare they have met, is God? And how can we be sure of finding him if we seek for him? The two questions have one answer: we cannot. Dead certainty, in any case, is dead. We are free to decide soberly and responsibly whether that Other shall be our God, and whether we shall identify ourselves as his creatures. We live by our decision to act upon our convictions, by our faith and not by incontestable evidence. It is especially important here that this be clearly understood, because most of us are not given (or perhaps are not yet capable of receiving) the kind of overwhelming assurance that is bestowed upon some individuals in the mystical vision, and in other experiences that have not been described in so much detail. When, after having prayed despairingly for our daily bread, we are nourished by a stranger's smile or the pattern of leaves against the sky, we must make up our minds whether to receive that sustenance as a gift from God or from some other source, or whether to take it as merely the beginning of a natural recovery from our mood. At that, however, we are not much worse off than the mystics. They also must decide whether they shall accept their vision as being from God, or as the product of — let us say — a physiological condition.

I have said earlier than Christianity is not essentially an intellectual system. Now it needs to be added that neither is it essentially dependent upon an emotional or "spiritual" or personal experience. If it were, those who are not naturally endowed with a passionate temperament, or who have been nurtured in less than ideal families, would face almost insuperable handicaps if they wished to become Christian. It is one thing, however, to say, "I have not seen God or experienced anything like 'a transcendent reality'," and another to conclude that therefore the reports made by others are invalid. The decisive error here is not that we deny a God but that in enthroning our own experience or lack of it, we repudiate not merely our neighbor's opinions but also his personal identity. As Charles Williams wrote of the Earl of Rochester, "God, his passion cried, did not reveal His secrets to men; for God, his pride added, had not revealed them to the Earl of Rochester."[2]

The question is whether we shall take our neighbor seriously as a person when his experience differs markedly from our own. If we do, we shall neither contemptuously dismiss his testimony nor defer credulously to his claims, but allow for him what we insist upon for ourselves: the right to see through his own eyes, to speak in his own words, and to understand the world in his own way, not in the way that we prescribe for him. In granting him the right to exist on his own terms, we acknowledge his integrity as an other, and prepare our — and his — way for recognizing the absolutely Other, just as the recognition of a divine Other equips us to admit and finally to love our neighbor's otherness.

The distance between those who affirm and those who deny a supernatural Other is as nothing compared to the distance between those who admit the authenticity and authority of any other, divine or human, and those who expect or require the experience and convictions of all others to conform with

49

their own. We know that what meets us is an other because it resists us, and it resists us because it is not like ourselves. When we grant it the right, as well as the power, to oppose us, our neighbor becomes our brother. When the sublimity of its difference arouses our wonder and worship, it becomes our Lord.

The Christian concept of God can be clarified further by examining briefly the objections most commonly raised by persons who argue against the belief in any God at all.

Some who reject the idea of God have pointed to the fact that the existence of a God cannot be fully and indisputably proved. The Christian agrees wholeheartedly, adding with what patience he can muster that nothing else can be proved, in that degree, either.

Some critics have inferred that because beliefs about and in gods produce feelings of stability, therefore the idea of God developed and persists in order to satisfy man's wish for security. The Christian again agrees with the observation but disagrees with the inference. We do need a feeling of security and belief in a God can help to provide it. But the fact of the need does not imply that the universe contains nothing which can meet that need, as if reality were intrinsically sordid, bleak, cold, and indifferent. It may be, or it may not. Apparently some human needs and desires can be satisfied — e.g., the hunger for food. Others apparently cannot — e.g., the craving to have our own will all the time and in every circumstance. While belief in God can be a form of wish-fulfilment for some persons, it can certainly be something quite different for other persons, even perhaps an accurate description of the world. The evidence for a God who exists independently of our desires or projections is obviously not conclusive, but the argument that because we need him he does not exist is both untenable and irrelevant.

It has been noted that people have tended to explain natural events that were mysterious to them, like earthquakes and the motion of the stars, by referring to a God, but that many of those phenomena can now be explained without reference to any deity. The Christian agrees yet again. Indeed, he may go farther than most scientists would today by suggesting that in due time all natural occurrences, without exception, can be understood without appealing to any action of any God. And then he can well ask what difference that would make. Whatever may be true of other religions, the Christian God is not a *deus ex machina*, interjected to answer questions about how nature operates or why it operates as it does. If and when all natural phenomena, all experiences, and all "miracles" have been explained entirely without reference to a God, or so as to exclude him, man's situation with respect to that belief will remain exactly what it is now. Both materialist and theist will continue to stand upon the presupposition that sense-perception, reasoning, and authorities are fairly reliable sources of truth, but not absolutely verifiable, and probably both will appeal to much the same evidence to sustain their opposite conclusions about God. But they will arrange the evidence to form different patterns. So man will continue to confront at least two defensible alternatives and will have to choose — will be free to choose — between them.

Many critics of the belief in God declare that believers have closed their minds, and thus have limited their freedom of intellectual investigation. Of course they have. Any belief whatsoever limits investigation and restricts the mind, including belief in the elementary proposition, "Some things are more important than others," or in its converse, "All things are equally important". The only fully open mind is *ipso facto* empty or chaotic. We close our minds when we assume "I think" or "I am", or that ideas are related to each other or to things in a reliable manner, and when we give names to things, and when we define words. We can change our beliefs or we can hold them skeptically, but we cannot think without them and every single one of them circumscribes our intellectual liberty.

One of the consequences of that restriction has special importance for Christian theology. Since we have no absolute guarantee of the truth of our presuppositions and inferences, we cannot be compelled by irrefutable evidence or argument. The finite nature of man at once forces us to choose what we shall believe, and believe in, and frees us to choose them. We are free to determine how we shall understand ourselves, life, and the world. Certainly our freedom has limits. For example, the evidence for the identity of my parents is so strong that I have no real choice in deciding whether to acknowledge them as my father and mother. Practically speaking, I am not free to deny that I am their child. The evidence that God is in any sense my father, however, is far from conclusive. He does not present irresistible testimony that would force me into admitting the relationship. Experience and reason will support either alternative; therefore I am free to believe that I am or am not a child of God.

Our freedom is also limited in two other ways that must be mentioned here. First, we cannot elect an option that we do not know about. Isaiah and Virgil could not be Christians because they lived before Christianity took shape. Second, some of the theoretical options are self-defeating. A person who chooses to be entirely self-reliant must refuse to accept food, drink, and even air from the world around him, and he will die. But so far as belief in God is concerned, Christianity traditionally has insisted that man is and must always remain free to decide for or against him. It says that we cannot escape choosing: our freedom stems from the nature of God, of the universe, of man himself. It declares that absolute, ultimate, and irrefutable proof of God's being and nature would destroy our freedom, so that in the end it is by the will of God that we cannot prove the truth or falsity of Christianity or any of its alternatives.

Critics of theism have pointed out that people and groups who do predicate a God disagree violently on what his nature and functions are. How can we argue from this, asks the Christian, that therefore all are equally wrong? To do so is to repeat the mistake of the legendary blind men with the elephant, who concluded that since their individual perceptions of the beast were contradictory, the elephant did not exist.

The Christian does not ignore the differences among religions. If anything, he stresses them in order to preserve their integrity as well as his own. Then he says, "I believe Christianity is right and the others are wrong." He should, of course, be tactful: he might say, "I prefer my beliefs to yours." He should be just: "Your way has valuable insights that I ought to know more about." He should be intelligent: "You adopted your beliefs and practices for sound reasons. In presenting my position, I shall take full account of them and of the reasons why Christianity may not commend itself to you." He should be accurate: "On some points we agree, although we use those doctrines in different ways and therefore they mean different things to us." But however we state our belief, and whatever the qualifications dictated by courtesy and willingness to learn, we cannot finally escape the fact that if the Christian view of the world is correct, those of other religions are wrong.

This bluntness will offend many, especially those who habitually confuse a soft heart with a soft head. But one can be committed to a belief without damning those who have committed themselves to a different belief and without concluding that those others are stupid or contemptible. One can hold his own in a disagreement without anger, discourtesy, or injustice. But unless he does believe, and believe in, his avowed position, Christian or otherwise, it is not his true position but only a figment of his self-deception. We accept a faith because we believe it to be true, and therefore we must believe that contradictory beliefs are false.

In recent years it has become fashionable to hold that believing oneself to be right and others wrong is a sign of intolerance, while tolerance consists of saying — in defiance of both logic and ordinary good sense — "I am right, but you are right, too." These interpretations debase two excellent words, and discourage the virtues that tolerance and intolerance, properly understood, refer to. One is intolerant when he refuses another the right and opportunity to exist. He is tolerant when he grants that right and opportunity to persons and ideas with whom he disagrees. Tolerance is not a name for inconclusiveness or indecision or evasion, much less for the pretense that all our disparities are superficial. It arises from the lively conviction that we are men and not gods. We believe ourselves to be right, but not that our rightness justifies us in ignoring or scorning or destroying persons who hold other beliefs.

Because this definition of tolerance combines conviction with humility, it makes tolerance a more difficult virtue than it usually appears to be. In addition, it restores intolerance to its proper place as a virtue. There are some things that our convictions should persuade us not to tolerate, some things that we should not permit to happen. Genocide may be one of them; torture may be another. The immediate point is not to locate the limits upon tolerance, but to stress that any deeply held conviction will impose limits upon tolerance, and should.

Finally, it is sometimes said that because it is as reasonable, or as unreasonable, to deny God as to have faith in him, the only principle on which decision can be made is personal preference, which is outside the scope of rational argument. Personal preference is indeed a manifestation of irrational factors, but to be irrational is not necessarily to be unreasonable, as we tacitly admit when we beg someone to "be reasonable", meaning not "Be objective, logical; see the situation in abstract terms," but "Be practical, be intelligent enough to see that reality is richer than pure reason and more flexible than the laws of syllogisms." Preference may be autocratic, but it is not inherently capricious or unenlightened. It is the expression of the whole person acting as a whole — in his integrity if he is integrated, or in his disintegrity.

We are so made that either we have a center of integrity or we become disintegrated. Moreover, we are free to choose whether our center shall be within or beyond ourselves, and so whether we shall develop in a centripetal or centrifugal direction, toward alienation or citizenship, and if a citizen, of what city. Shall we try to draw all men into ourselves, judge them by their conformity with ourselves, impose our intentions upon them, coerce them into serving our vocations? There are occasions when we can legitimately make such demands while still reverencing the otherness of others. If, however, our center is in a wholly Other and we wholly submit to him, we shall become participants in a life that is other than our own. The Other can be a God or group of gods, a beloved person or institution or cause, money or power, but the enlargement that follows such participation will depend upon the comprehensiveness of that other. Most of us try out many centers before we find one that is capable of enlightening our minds, satisfying our hearts, and bringing all our contradictions and complexities into a stable, but not static, integrity.

Chapter 5

GOD THE

PREPOSITIONS, CONJUNCTIONS, AND ARTICLES CAN BE DECISIVELY SIG-nificant in theological discourse, just as they are in ordinary writing and speech. "God is *a* something" implies that this something is one of his characteristics, or that he is only one of the many who possess it. "God is *the* something" affirms that he is unique in possessing it, or that it belongs to him in a singular way or degree. At this point and by means of the word "the", the Apostles' Creed answers the question whether the Other to which it is directed shall be, for the Christian, the only ultimate center or one within a range of several possible centers. It says that God is *the* Father and Maker of all things.

Chapter 6

GOD THE FATHER

THE WORDS FATHER, ALMIGHTY, AND MAKER ARE ALL CONCERNED
with the specific nature of the Other in whom Christians believe.
What do they believe about him? What do they claim to know
about him? Formulas like the Apostles' and other creeds supply
model answers to such questions; thus they do not need to be
understood as implying that any deviation from the model is
un-Christian, anti-Christian, or pre-Christian. Occasionally in the
history of the Christian community, the creeds have been employed as restrictive definitions of what all Christians must
believe, as if one did not deserve the name Christian until he
had reached the City of God and had already begun to live in
it. What we are considering here, however, is Christianity as
a process, a movement, a journey of individuals and groups
who are distinguished as Christian or non-Christian by their
orientation, not by their achievement. So it is equally appropriate — and in these times much more useful — to admit that
where we are is en route, and that the Creed is bequeathed to
us by our predecessors to tell us what we can expect to find
if we persist in following the road to the City of the Christian
God.

The ascription "Father" can suggest so many things that its
basic meaning is likely to be smothered in its connotations.
Fundamentally, it does not refer to affection or authority or
provision for a family's needs. What it centrally and inescap-
ably means is production. A father begets offspring. He gener-
ates descendants. After the progenitive act, he can abandon
his mate and any offspring they may have conceived, and never
know or care what becomes of them. Still he remains the father
of his children. Therefore, "God is a father" means that God

is a source from which other things are derived. If he is the Father, then everything that exists is directly or indirectly derived from him.

Since we are in a solidly defensible position when we interpret God's paternity in terms of derivation, it is important for us to examine carefully the process of derivation itself. The most obvious instances are sexual reproduction in plants, animals, and men. We look farther and see that all living beings derive sustenance from the world about them, and that many organisms die in providing food for other organisms. Looking in another direction, we derive most of our ideas from other persons. We learn from our families and teachers and friends, from books and the cultures in which we live. We give help: we allow others to be derived from us. We accept help: we consent to be derived from them. Derivation is essential for life on all levels, from the cellular to the spiritual. Physically, biologically, intellectually, personally, socially, we may or may not choose to live for one another, but we do live from one another and from nature. We are continuously accepting derivation from powers and entities that we did not create and cannot entirely control.

Because these others resist us, we know them to be outside ourselves. They exist independently of our desires, and most of them appear to be indifferent to our welfare. The resistance may be purely physical, as when the floor prevents us from falling through it to the ground beneath. It may be mental, as when a new idea attacks our established beliefs and we are happily surprised or horridly shocked. Those of us who are not completely integrated will astonish ourselves, agreeably or disagreeably, when one part of our selves resists another part. But only that which resists us can support us.[3] The doctrine of the fatherhood of God, therefore, as it defines the source from whom man and nature are derived, refers precisely to the Other who is known to us in the resistance and support that we receive in every phase of our existence and development.

We can credit this Other with being natural or divine, and closer than hands and feet or farther than the stars, and either position can be a station on the way to the other. The fact that we are resisted and supported can be admitted dully as a commonplace matter of fact, or in such amazement that we worship its glory as some of our ancestors did — and some of our contemporaries do. But when the Christian calls God his Father, he is not necessarily displaying an emotional response or assuming an emotion on the part of God. Rather, he is acknowledging the existence of a relationship that he may enjoy or dislike, as any of us may be involved in pleasant or unpleasant relationships that we cannot escape. Our emotional responses do not invariably determine the content of our beliefs. We can hate and fear death without denying its reality. We can delight in beauty without asserting its objective existence. The Creed says "I believe in God the Father" without prescribing that the belief must be eager or happy, and without requiring that the believer pretend to an enthusiasm which he does not spontaneously feel, or that he hide his impulsive distaste for doctrines or events or activities that repel him. The critical factor is the faith produced by thought and decision, and issuing in action — in Charles Williams' terms, what our intelligences lead us to decide to believe is the nature of the universe.[4] How we feel about our faith is another matter — important, to be sure, but different, and not relevant at this stage in our deliberations.

Many people today object to describing God as a father on the grounds that it implies an anthropomorphic deity, and depends for its effectiveness upon an analogy which is no longer meaningful. The answer to both objections starts from the observation that nothing produced by derivation is either intrinsically alien to its source or identical with its source. A poem bears the imprint of the poet but poem and poet are not the same thing. A wisely loving parent knows that his child is part of his inmost self but that at the same time the child is utterly apart from, even foreign to, himself. Daily the bereaved cry out, "A part of myself has died!" and here language may lead us astray. We sometimes think that the part can be identified, but it cannot. Our elemental loves and griefs affect the entire person, in the same way that the good or bad performance of the heart affects the entire body.

Thus if, as Christianity has declared, the ultimate origin of man is the Other who is God the Father, we need not be ashamed or dismayed to find ourselves portraying God in our own image, rather than in the image of a machine or a vast inhuman energy or a rock or tree. The anthropomorphic strain in Christianity cannot be denied. But the Christian does not need to deny it or to gloss it over because anthropomorphism, rightly understood, is not a weakness but a strength, a witness to a great and terrible truth. Like most other truths, anthropomorphism frequently appears in dark forms, as when men deify their malice or ruthlessness or ambition for power. But the core of the Christian declaration remains. We are not gods, but being derived from God, we are like him. Therefore it is fitting that we should conceive of him in images taken from that which is most central to our experience: ourselves as persons.

Certain other religions teach the irreconcilable disparity between God and man. For some of them, God is a force or an All-Soul or an absolute which cannot be compared with anything human because it is incompatible with humanity. From the Christian viewpoint, these religions have grasped one aspect of the truth, that God is indeed the absolutely Other, the extreme opposite of the entire created universe. Then by a movement of thought that defies logic and comes straight from the nearly universal experience of mankind, Christian doctrine fuses that insight with its own by saying that God is essentially like man, as a father is like his child, and unlike man as a father is different from his child.

The difference-in-likeness is illustrated in another way by the analogy between the fatherhood of God and human fathers, who throughout all the ages have been notoriously defective images of God. It is generally recognized that children need father-images, and intensive efforts are made in our society to provide them for children whose natural fathers are absent. It is less widely appreciated that all our lives we need fathering and therefore father-images, because we need the authoritative resistance and support that supply substantial body to the framework within which we live. All human images must fail, not only because they are human, but also because images function successfully by their failures. A perfectly adequate image or symbol or analogy would persuade us to focus our attention on it, instead of directing our vision through and beyond it. By means of its imperfection, we begin to discern what perfection might be. So we need not one father-image, but a succession of them, each known to be temporary and partial, but each providing a new embodiment of authority and a new vision, until we see the Father himself face to face.

"I believe in God the Father," the Other from whom I am derived and upon whom I ultimately depend. It is no easier to trust the divine Father than to trust the love of a parent who subjects us to unwelcome restrictions, or the good will of a friend whose opinions conflict with ours, or the devotion of a lover who fails to answer a letter by return mail, or the wisdom of a physician who prescribes a severe remedy for a disease that is not yet disabling. In such commonplace situations, we learn how to believe in. We exercise our capacity for faith. Here we should learn also to correct and discipline our faith. Undiscriminating trust is a dead-end street, intellectually, morally, emotionally, physically, and spiritually, and a very short street at that. What would happen to our minds if we consistently believed everything we heard or read, or to our bodies if we swallowed everything we could put into our mouths? We must evaluate and test and explore if we are to know what the fatherhood of God means now, or has meant, or may come to mean when we have gone beyond the minimum to the heights that the saints and the great theologians record.

Chapter 7

GOD THE FATHER ALMIGHTY

THE QUESTION ANSWERED BY THE WORD "ALMIGHTY" IS THAT OF the scope within which the ultimate Other functions, the extent and limits of God's power. The Christian believes himself to be a derivative and dependent being, having his source in an Other whom he has met or believes that he will meet. Then rejecting the possibility that in these respects he is set apart from the remainder of the natural world, he goes on to say that all other persons and things are also derived from and dependent upon this same God.

No exceptions. The subconscious is as much under his dominion as the stars. Any life on other planets is derived from, and resisted and supported by, this God. Any supernatural, arch-natural, preternatural, and unnatural modes of being are established and sustained by him. The entire universe is derived from one source and exhibits one order. It operates by one set of co-ordinated principles and it has one purpose and end. All our knowledge, art, and religion, as well as our everyday life, reflect in their own ways a totally integrated world.

We shall be able to see more plainly what is involved here if we compare this view of the world with another that is currently popular, which sees man as partially divided from nature. It insists that man is the product of nature, but it goes on to say that in producing man nature outdid herself, with the result that now man is capable of transcending nature. Specifically, he can order his experiences into meaningful patterns, and so direct his activities that he can even control the direction of future evolution by genetic, educational, and social methods.

The obstacle for the Christian in this view is the discontinuity it imposes between man and the rest of the universe. By asserting man's transcendence over nature, the proponents of this doctrine imply a double world, of thought and everything else, and a double set of laws, rational and physical, the one goal-directed and meaningful, the other mechanical and meaningless. Worse, they locate the division within man himself. His body is said to belong to one world, and his intellectual, volitional, and perhaps his emotional constituents to the other.

In contrast, the Christian tradition declares the unity of the whole man with the whole of nature, and of nature with God, so that Christians have historical grounds for refusing to tolerate a fundamental split in man, or between man and nature, or between nature and God. They can affirm, for example, that man's disposition to see order and purpose in things is evidence for — not against — the existence of meaning in the universe of which he is an integral part. So far as we know, man is more aware of the patterns in his experience than are the so-called lower animals, although our techniques for exchanging information with them and with non-living beings are so limited that we have no conclusive evidence as to the extent of our superiority to them on this score. Neither do we have clear evidence concerning beings who may be superior to us, but we have no warrant for claiming positively, in the absence of demonstration, that no such creatures inhabit time or space or eternity.

If we presuppose a single order in all things, then we must give the same weight to psychological and spiritual evidence, such as that for purposiveness, as we give the logical and physical evidence against purposiveness. Further, we can expect that knowledge of ourselves as persons will contribute at least as much to our understanding of other forms of being as our study of them has contributed to our knowledge of ourselves. But are there any principles — is there even one principle — that applies so directly both to man-as-person and to the remainder of the universe that we can see and perhaps test the existence of such a single order?

The one which seems to me most immediately evident is the process variously named "interdependence" or "co-inherence"

63

or "exchange", and most clearly explained in the writings of Charles Williams. As he points out, all existence is dependent upon acts of exchange. Every form and level of life about which we know anything at all depends for its origin and continuation upon some form of giving and receiving, acting and resting, inhaling and exhaling, ingesting and egesting, accepting and rejecting, believing and disbelieving. Likewise the inorganic realm depends upon exchange, although less obviously to the naked eye, and I shall leave it to the physicists to describe the exchanges of energy among subnuclear entities and fields of force, and their role in producing what we call "matter". Here it is important only to note that exchange is as characteristic of this realm as of the organic and the personal.

Further, all the arts result from the interaction of observation and expression. Societies are arrangements by which men, singly and in groups, exchange the products of their labor for the products of others' labors. Peace results from a balance of exchanges, war from their imbalance. Beings become persons by interacting with other persons. The most precise definition of sanctity is free and full interchange with God, and in the concept of derivation we see manifested that co-inherence which is one of the results of exchange. Still further, good and evil can be defined in terms of exchange, the good being that which facilitates or increases the exchanges, and evil that which inhibits or perverts them. What particular acts are good or evil, by this definition, will vary widely with circumstances: conceivably, monogamy in one culture and polygamy in another, and certainly at one time silence and another speech.

As the principle of gravitation covers and unites widely diverse and sometimes contrary forms of action — the rising of a helium-filled balloon and the falling of an apple — so the principle of exchange is fulfilled in a multitude of different activities. It is the precondition for existence and the goal of morality, the foundation of societies and the definition of love. It asserts the fact of our interdependence, and it leads to two additional observations, one broad in its purview, the other narrower but of immense practical importance.

Beings must be different from each other before they can

exchange at all. A fish can live by eating other fish but not by eating itself. We can learn only from persons whose ideas are different from our own. If one breathes the same air over and over, he will suffocate. Difference is essential to life. "The holy and glorious flesh" illustrates this principle admirably. The body is composed of a variety of structures, and it cannot live, much less flourish, unless each part performs adequately its unique function. We need hearts as well as stomachs, arteries as well as glands. Cellular function depends upon cellular structure. Muscles cannot do their proper work unless they are firmly connected to bones or other supports. The different structures and functions, however, are not separate. Even anatomically, we cannot dissociate respiration from circulation when we describe the lungs, or circulation from digestion when dealing with the liver, or muscles from nerves and bones in considering bodily motion. The differences are as vital as the interconnections. Without the diversity within the union, and the union of diversities, there could be no life in our bodies.

It is axiomatic in biology that since all the physiological functions and their respective anatomical structures are necessary for life, they are equally important. This does not mean, however, that the same degree of activity will be required of each from moment to moment, or even from day to day. Under some circumstances, eating is more important for the health of the organism than sleeping; at other times, it will be imperative to rest rather than to eat. In a city, the collection of garbage can well be a more pressing need than provision for higher education: a people ridden with filth-borne disease will not have the physical capacity for sustained study. It may require education to demonstrate the connection between sanitation and intellectual achievement — which brings us back to the theme of the interdependence among heterogeneous functions. If short-term needs be ignored, we do not survive for the long term. If long-term needs be ignored, we collapse into the fragmentation that results from attending only to details.

Within the co-inherent structure of exchange, the problem is not how to establish a consistent and stable pattern in which every part keeps its place, but how to foster each other's diversities so that we continually exchange places, each exalting the others' uniqueness and being exalted by them. Thus the social reformer might honor the contemplative for praying instead of urging him to political activity, and the contemplative might bless the reformer in his work instead of exhorting him to fast and pray. Patriarchs might rejoice in the brief, fiery extravagance of the young, and the young might learn to be grateful for the steadiness of the old that provides the framework for their rebellion. As we willingly co-inhere with one another, our unity and diversity are simultaneously enhanced. We do not, however, create the co-inherence. It is given to us, rooted in the foundations of the world, and there is no escape from it except through death, if then.

The principle of co-inherent exchange also has momentous implications for the doctrine of man. It undercuts a belief about man that has permeated Western thought since the time of the classic Greek philosophers, and perhaps earlier: that "body" on the one hand, and "soul" or "spirit" or "essence" on the other, are separate entities, divisible or even incompatible by nature. The picture given by the pattern of co-inherence is that of the person as a single entity, equally dependent upon body, mind, and spirit as the living body is equally dependent upon all its structures and functions. Some of these aspects of the person are visible (e.g., his color, shape, motion) ; some are hidden from the eye but perceptible by other means (e.g., his weight, temperature, acuity of hearing) ; still others are clearly discernible only to himself (e.g., his memories) or only to other persons (e.g., the impression he makes upon them). He is a complex unity wherein the activity of every part influences every other part, and where acquaintance with any part can give access to the whole —"The body through the mind; the mind through the body."[5] Yet no part can be understood except through its activity within the whole.

The widespread belief that man is essentially spirit, with the body a prison or garment or illusion, is not Christian but pagan and has repeatedly been condemned by Christian churches and theologians as a heresy. The Gnostic form of that heresy has plagued the Christian faith from its earliest days with the notion that spirit as such is intrinsically important and good while body is intrinsically unimportant and probably evil. Gnosticism is still prevalent among us under the aegis of Christianity, manifesting itself in a thousand subtle ways. Thus there are many who affirm staunchly that Jesus was fully man yet who are repelled by the suggestion that he may sometimes have suffered from digestive distress or even a cold in the head. We speak of "spiritual values" as if that kind of value were in a class all by itself. The coarse doctrines of a fleshly resurrection and a real heaven are so offensive to many churchmen and some ministers and theologians that they openly reject them, at times bolstering their conclusion with an interpretation of St. Paul abandoned by most biblical scholars long ago. And some of the opposition to the Christian belief that God created the world stems from the feeling, too deeply ingrained to be called a thought, that it is beneath the dignity of a God to associate himself with such grossly material activities and things.

The Christian asserts the unity of body and spirit not as an evasive way of subjugating one to the other, but in order to make utterly clear that both are necessary to the human person, that they are different manifestations of one reality, and that they are inseparable. At times, obviously, our bodies are at war with our minds and our minds with our bodies. We are divided beings, still disintegrated, still unhealed. But Christianity says that our humanity is fulfilled and perfected not through a more intense conflict — separating the mind or soul from the body — but by integrating all the different aspects of our being into one complex system of processes that guards and enhances the individual identity of its parts.

This description of the nature of man not only implies that exchange is necessary if we are to exist, but also leaves us free to choose our attitude toward that necessity, and to determine how far beyond the minimum we shall go toward fulfilling our humanity. We can seek to interact with increasing depth and range with other beings, or we can strive to give but not to receive, or to receive but not to give, or to alienate ourselves from all the exchanges of life that we can manage to avoid. These last three, however, are denials of the basis of life. They are ways out of exchange into death.

Nothing in the foregoing discussion of exchange is peculiar to Christianity or has been discovered under the influence of Christianity. The exchanges occur on the level of nature, and the laws of exchange operate as stringently and as precisely upon unbelievers as upon believers. All things naturally participate in exchange, just as all bodies on this earth are influenced by gravitation. A man who falls off the top of a skyscraper does not break the law of gravitation: he illustrates it. Equally, the man who resists exchanging is shattered completely and surely, although not always swiftly or spectacularly. It required extraordinary insight to formulate the principles of gravitation and exchange into a comprehensive system, but they function independently of our information or convictions about them.

Therefore, as we should expect, many religious groups and some unreligious and antireligious ones hold similar views of the world. Since human beings are subject to the laws of exchange, they will enjoy more efficient and pleasant interpersonal relationships if they obey the Golden Rule than if they flout it, just as fire will cook and warm more efficiently and comfortably if it is confined within a stove. But such likenesses as these are not signs that we all worship the same God or that all religions are fundamentally alike. A God who offers his devotees a salvation from their bodies and absorption into an impersonal absolute that obliterates their self-consciousness and individual identity, cannot be the same God who promises them a salvation that encompasses the body and heightens their individual sensitivity and responsiveness. The alternatives proposed by the major religions of the world are not compatible; and eclectics, picking from every tradition whatever they happen to like, merely corrupt what is best in each by snatching it out of its appropriate context. They prostrate themselves before the shadow of shadows.

What is unique to Christianity is the conviction that the acts of exchange are not only natural, but are also holy. They are both necessary and divine, both the inexorable law of nature and the glory of God's love. By the natural processes of obser-

vation and thought, we can discover the compulsions of interchange and even its pleasures; we cannot discern its holiness
except as God reveals it to us. Natural piety and natural theology deserve our honor. They are partial truths by which man
learns to be at home in nature. But Christianity declares that
nature herself, in all her material actuality, is at home in God.

In relating nature to God through the principle of exchange,
the Christian sets nature within a larger context where impersonal natural law becomes one of the manifestations of personal divine will. The rigor of natural laws is seen as exhibiting what the Bible calls the faithfulness of God: his strict con-
sistency in his covenant with his creation. On this premise, it
is no more "interference" for God to act within the world
than it is "interference" when gravitation affects the motion
of a stone, or the eye affects seeing, or a person initiates a personal encounter or responds to a personal request. These forms
of exchange are what constitute the relationship. Far from being
intrusions, they are its essence, the conditions under which the
theoretical possibility becomes an effectual relationship, and
without them there would be no relationship at all.

If this view of the universe is correct, we live in a highly
integrated world, sometimes directing our attention to the problems and activities we call "scientific", at another time restrict-
ing our attention to those we call "aesthetic", or enlarging our
vision to include the whole pattern when we create theologies,
or relating ourselves entirely to that whole in our religious cele-
brations. There are no walls around these areas of our concern,
although there is a great difference in emphasis, and a single
person can engage in several of them simultaneously. There is,
however, an all but impenetrable barrier between those to whom
the world is inclusively integrated, and those who are content
with two or more autonomous worlds.

The unity implied in "the Father Almighty" brings together
our reflections upon the world and our experience within the
world. Accepting it, we affirm both our bondage to necessity,
and the power of God to transform our necessity into freedom.
We enfold the concept of repetitive impersonal process within
the massive sphere of flexible personal will, and within both

69

we find the exchanges that are decreed by the personal God who is the source of everything that is. Admitting the need for logical coherence, we affirm the greater need for personal integration.

The Hebrews, and after them the Christians, took the steps that lead to integrity, from "the God who resists and supports me" to "he is resisting and supporting all that is", and from "he is the source of all life and meaning" to "he is the source of my life and meaning". They united themselves irrevocably with nature and history by uniting themselves with God. They did not arrogate to themselves a fundamental way of life that they denied to other creatures, nor did they claim for themselves an unparalleled centrality or eminence. They did claim that the nature of the universe, including their own nature, reflects the nature of God, so that he who is obedient to the will of God *ipso facto* lives in conformity with the demands of nature, intellect, art, and spiritual growth. To know God is to know things as they are, and they are vitally related to one another because they are vitally related to the God who is Almighty.

Chapter 8

GOD THE FATHER ALMIGHTY, MAKER

FOR A GOOD MANY YEARS, THE LIVELIEST DEBATES ABOUT GOD AS Maker centered on the doctrine of biological evolution, and ran something like this: "We know that man evolved from lower forms of life; to say that a God guided the process, or set it going, adds nothing to our understanding of it, and breaks one of the most valuable rules of good thinking: do not multiply concepts unnecessarily." This is an argument with which many Christians fully agree. But it misses the point. The Christian doctrine of creation is not primarily an answer to the rational scientific inquiry, "Where did man and the universe come from, and how did they get to be what they are?" Instead, it is grounded in wonder, and directed to the importunate question of whether we are at the disposal of a mechanical or fortuitous Destiny, or subject to a divine Will. Do we just happen to exist or were we intentionally made? These questions can best be approached through a discussion of meaninglessness and meaning.

To treat different theories of creation and evolution as if the Christian faith depended upon choosing rightly among them is to be at best irrelevant and at worst frivolous. Even the creation stories in Genesis describe what God does and not how he does or did it, or why. Modern scholars have accumulated strong evidence from anthropology, linguistics, history, and other disciplines for their conviction that the Hebrews were passionately concerned about God's relationships with them — that he upheld and led them — and were so little interested in his methods of working in nature that occasionally they made gross errors in describing natural phenomena. In spite of the Levitical injunction, neither the rock badger nor the hare chews a cud. The Genesis tales of creation say essentially what Psalm 104 says, and that is a paean to the Lord who is doing wonderful things now, like causing grass to grow for the cattle to eat, and who has made the world sufficiently stable that we can rest assured of his faithfulness to his creation and his delight in it as long as the world lasts. The narrators of the Genesis stories decorated their theme with a plot and characters, as has been the way of man ever since the first times of which we have record. It is their — and our — misfortune that interpreters who came out of another tradition have pushed aside the meat of the narratives while they savored critically the sauce with which it was garnished.

Like the Hebrews, Christians have traditionally grounded their faith on the astounding realization that things might have happened differently. If we — as mankind or as our particular selves — might very well have not existed at all, or have existed in some drastically different form, then everything which does exist becomes an occasion for wonder. A geneticist has told me that the chances are no better than one in at least a billion or two that a given sexual union will result in an Augustine or a Napoleon, or you or me. The probability that any of us would come into being is so remote as to make our presence in the world incredible. Yet here we are, and there Napoleon and Augustine were. Likewise, the exercise of our respective freedoms, not to mention the freedoms of our progenitors, associates, and mentors, plus the impact upon us all of a multitude of necessities, has brought me to writing this sentence and you to reading it at this one exact moment in each of our lives — a fantastically unlikely and unpredictable eventuality.

The doctrine that God is the maker of all things reflects the awesome fact that we and this beautiful and terrible world do exist. It has nothing to say about the probability that we should, or its predictability, or the manner in which it all happened. It is the Christian's expression of astonished wonder at the wild concatenation of events that has resulted in himself and his world. He declares, in this doctrine, not a hypothesis about sources or modes of operation — evolution, predeterminism, or whatever — but an awareness of the world that exists within and

around him. And he acknowledges gladly the enlightenment he
has received from scientists into the processes by which an infinite multiplicity of chances and choices has led to the existence
of these specific events and unique persons whom he knows, out
of the illimitable number of others which might have occurred
instead.

Out of our wonder rises the conviction that we ourselves,
and the universe we live in, have a meaning. No intellectual
operations can demonstrate that the incredible number and
variety of the things we know — not to mention the things we
do not know — are related to one another in such a way as
to make a meaningful pattern in which each separate element
has a significant place. The fact that almost universally men
have ascribed such a meaning to existence proves nothing about
the nature of the world, although it does say much about the
nature of man — who is a part of that world.

There is a stupendous gulf between "Life has no meaning,
or at most only such meaning as man imposes upon it," and
"Life itself has a meaning whether man recognizes it or not,
and whatever he does or leaves undone." The believer in meaninglessness supposes, on the basis of good evidence, that no
meaning exists to be discovered. He predicates that the universe is a dead end. The Christian, on equally good evidence,
supposes that there is enough reason to believe in a meaning
that the possibility deserves to be investigated. He does not —
or he should not — categorically maintain that the existence of
a meaning can be conclusively proved, but only that the evidence is sufficiently persuasive to justify his search for it. Or at
the very least, he can say that the evidence does not warrant
the blanket refusal to consider the hypothesis.

The issue here is not between one meaning in contrast to
another, but between any inherent meaning as opposed to none.
The opponents do not always agree on what evidence should
be admitted as valid and relevant. One party to the debate
declares that the relevant evidence includes man's wonder, his
seemingly ineradicable impulse to seek for causes and relationships, his profound impression that there is order and meaning
in things themselves and not merely in his own mind. The

other excludes, so far as possible, such responses and tendencies of man as if they were somehow apart from nature, unnatural.

Do we impose meaning upon what we observe, or do we discover meaning within it? No answer to that question will affect any scientific finding or hypothesis or dogma in the slightest. It is not the authority of science which is at stake, but its autonomy: the relation between the scientific kingdom and the empire of man's total knowledge and concern, in other words, the context within which the facts and interpretations of science are to be placed. This matter is critical, because meanings always depend upon contexts. An idea such as biological evolution will mean one thing to a devout believer in man's supremacy over nature, and something else to a devout believer in man's subordination to God. Within the specialized context of scientific explanation, the concept of a creating and sustaining God is an intrusive irrelevance. Within the comprehensive context of our lives as persons, with our sense of dependence and our awe as we behold the world, recognition of this God becomes entirely appropriate.

The damage that has been done by failures to admit the validity of different contexts for different purposes is immeasurable and tragic. Most theologians today admit the authority of science to be supreme in its own place, its own context. They deny that its place is above all other places, and that its context is all-inclusive. The fact that a question cannot be answered by scientific methods, or has no meaning within the scientific context, does not prevent it from being meaningful to persons and answerable by other methods. As the language analysts have repeatedly shown and as certain artists have strikingly displayed, isolated words are nonsense syllables; and ideas ripped from their contexts, and made to stand alone or set in an unfitting place, are deprived of whatever sense they may originally have had. It is not easy to determine how various contexts — kingdoms of thought — should be related to one another. What can the mystic learn from solid state physics that will speed his journey? When should the mathematician seek light on a mathematical problem from the artist or artisan? To which of the disciplines — intellectual, moral, aesthetic, personal — should we give the authority to order our exchanges? In practice, we take this authority upon ourselves, revealing in our manner of exercising it whether we conceive of ourselves as under obedience or as superior to any obedience, and whether we see the world as our fellow-creature or our slave.

But if the world is meaningful, and if we can discover the meaningful interactions of its kingdoms, we are still left with a formidable obstacle: the existence of evil. Theoretically and practically, it is as difficult and as important to account for good as for evil, but since the latter more often engages our attention, I shall limit this discussion to that aspect of the total problem.

The concept of God as the omnipotent creator is easy enough to live with if one declares that he is not good, no matter how goodness is defined, or that he is morally neutral. And "God is good" can be affirmed without particular difficulty so long as one believes that he did not create and does not have the power to prevent the brutalities, corruptions, frustrations, and agonies that constantly affront us. To reasonable and well-meaning persons, it may seem obvious that a good God would not have confused the meaning of his world with the sufferings of the innocent, the destruction of irreplaceable beauty, perversions of truth, and all the other horrors that threaten and engulf us. Yet Christians have always claimed that he is both good and almighty, that he and he alone is the source of our existence and meaning, and that the world does in fact contain innumerable and unutterable evils.

Traditionally, one of the major ways of uniting these incompatibles has been to accept one specific limit upon the omnipotence of God, and then to define goodness as being independent of our likes and dislikes, pleasures and pains, desires and repugnances, insights and stupidities.

The one restriction upon God's omnipotence that has been generally assumed by Christians is that set by his own nature. He is said to be personal, not in the pejorative sense of eccentric, capricious, biased, unreliable, or irresponsible, but in the sense that he has personal integrity and is therefore consistent, dependable, faithful. He deliberately maintains the order that he

built into his creation, making rain to fall on the just and
unjust together or withholding it impartially from both. His
goodness prevents him from doing or willing evil. His love bars
him from hate or contempt or vindictiveness toward his creation. His integrity does not allow any disintegrity or disintegration to exist within himself or to be expressed in his actions.
"In him is no darkness at all."

"What is good?" rings with the same haunting note as "What
is truth?" It is hard enough to deal with the question in relation to general standards, worse to cope with it in specific situations. At least, however, we have one firm starting point. All
societies and cultures known to us, and nearly all individuals,
call some things good and others evil. Their criteria range from
"the general welfare" to "whatever I happen to want", and
from "it depends entirely upon the local circumstances" to "thus
saith the Lord". But the fact that they do have ethical standards
of some sort is far more revealing than the variation in content
among those standards.

The Christian definition of the good is easy to state: the
good is what God wills. That is, the ultimate standard is not
established by men, and even such widely accepted goals as
social justice, eradication of poverty and disease, and freedom
with peace, must be measured against a standard of goodness
that is not chosen by man but exists in the nature of things as
they are ordained by God. Therefore the question for Christians
is not, "Is a particular action reasonable, or creative, or practical,
or in conformity with this or that biblical text?" but "Is it the
will of God?" Our values are subject to God's judgement. Except
in a negative way, however, this gives us almost no help at all,
because we do not know — absolutely, ultimately, or irrefutably
— what the will of God is, and the preceding discussion of
knowledge indicates that we cannot, in this life at least, find
out with unconditional certainty what he wills.

It has already been pointed out that to deny our ability to
know perfectly does not necessarily lead to the conclusion that
we can know nothing, or that all knowledge is equally uncer-
tain or fallacious. Our position with respect to the knowledge
of good and evil is very much the same. We do make ethical

distinctions. We have no guarantee of their full and final correctness. And we are not only free to choose, we must choose the standards by which we shall judge specific situations and evaluate general approaches to ethics. Nothing in heaven or earth compels us to select the Christian standard. Everything in heaven and earth compels us to select some standard.

It may be intellectually tolerable to say that since only God knows what his will is, there is no inherent contradiction between his omnipotence and his goodness, but this conclusion offends our very being. What about his omnipotence in relation to those things which we feel in our bones are evil? Here we must distinguish between God's will and his permission. He creates and wills only good; he permits evil; and he makes it possible for any evil to be transformed into good, to be redeemed.

The Christian tradition begins its interpretation of evil by affirming the intrinsic goodness of the created world. But the exchanges that are at once the necessity for all existence and the means of grace can be arrested or corrupted. To some extent, interruptions of exchange appear to be built into the structure of the universe. For example, apart from a few minute organisms, no living creature can survive without preying upon other living creatures, animal or plant. One system must die in order that another may live. Each must kill if it is to live. Because these destructions are necessary, they cannot be classified as generically evil, although we may properly condemn a given instance of the lion slaying the lamb, as we might also properly condemn a lion's renunciation of his leonine nature if he were to espouse vegetarianism. Death and destruction are not evil in themselves. They become evil when they are not integrated within the pattern of co-inherent exchange, but distort or block its integrity.

Of the authentically evil disintegrations, some stem directly from the gift of freedom. An omnipotent God could have created beings who were incapable of twisting the good things of life into ignominy, who never misunderstood or were ignorant, who invariably willed his will, and who automatically converted their infallible knowledge and faultless intentions into sublimely appropriate action. But such beings would be puppets

— superbly beautiful puppets, no doubt, but still puppets. Freedom opens to man, and perhaps to other creatures, the possibility of doing either good or evil, and it lays upon him the responsibility for his decisions. Freedom of choice and action is a bitter gift. Often we would like to barter it for freedom from error. With our freedom, however, comes consolation. If our freedom was given to us by an almighty God, we are not responsible for having it in the first place, nor are we responsible for the uncertainty of our knowledge, the confusion in our motives, or our inability to act blamelessly. Our responsibility for ourselves and our world, real and pressing though it is, is limited as our knowledge and capacities are limited.

Thus we are released from the intolerable demand for perfection, and from the equally intolerable burden of having to bear on our human shoulders the whole weight of the world. We err from necessity, a situation that is at once humbling and liberating. We are humbled because our visions and powers outstrip our performance, and we culpably neglect responsibilities that we could fulfil. We are liberated because we are no longer crippled by futile efforts to do and be something alien to our human natures. When we cease trying to be gods, we can become completely ourselves. According to this thesis, God could not prevent us from committing evil without obliterating our freedom, and he has, it seems, determined that the mixed good and evil of free creatures is better than the morally neutral activity of puppets, that he would rather have free sons than slaves. He has been faithful to his choice through inquisitions, concentration camps, crucifixions; so far, he is to blame for them.

There are also the events, relationships, and things that strike us as unmistakably evil and that we can neither attribute to man's freedom nor explain by reference to any necessity for survival or growth. Babies suffering intractible pain from cancer. Epidemic starvation following a flood. Animals burning alive in a forest fire set by lightning. These bring us decisively to the core of the problem of evil. Why does an omnipotent God allow such atrocities to happen? How can a good God consent to evil?

We do not know. Here we must decide whether "We have

no answer" does or does not imply "There is no answer". "There is no answer" leads to despair. "There is an answer, although I do not know it" leads to hope. Earlier it was suggested that if man's intellect is part of the universe, it is reasonable to suppose that what satisfies his rational mind is likely to be closer to the truth than what affronts his intelligence. Now I suggest that man's heart is also part of the universe, and the despair which petrifies his heart is a less adequate response to life than the hope which intensifies his search for deeper understanding. And Christianity specifically and vehemently places man's hope in something other than his pitiful, magnificent, divided, striving self: in God. What saves the Christian from despair is not his conviction that he now knows or will sometime know the meaning of evil, but his assurance that God knows.

"You must always make your choice," wrote Charles Williams, "or always, at least know that the choice exists — all luck is good — or not."[6] Sooner or later, we shall be driven to accept all things as coming from the good and omnipotent God, or to conclude that nothing comes from him. We have here another either-or proposition, and this is the exact and inescapable point where we determine whether God in Christ is to be our Lord or a hypothetical possibility, and whether we will trust him or only trust in ourselves.

To accept as from God the tragic circumstances of our upbringing, the defects in our physical and mental equipment that cut us off forever from our hearts' desire, the flagrant injustices inflicted upon us by social maladjustments or ill-directed governments, the appalling results of disease, does not make any of them good in themselves. It does mean that by persistent and agonizing labor of the whole person — intellect, heart, body, and spirit — we can so unite ourselves with the power of God that we can discover good in them and create good from them. They can be brought into the pattern of exchange. They can be integrated with other events so as to become productive of good. They can be redeemed. These dreadful episodes cannot be erased from our lives and should not be erased from our minds. They exist, and to deny or palliate them is a lie.

79

But when we recognize them as material from which good can be made, when we know them as potential sources of glory, we can work with or upon them to bring them — and ourselves — effectively under the sovereignty of the almighty God who is the maker of *all* things.

Perhaps the most remarkable feature of the Christian concept of God as maker consists of its corollary, that the Omnipotence does not always exercise his omnipotence. The Creator submits to his creatures. He endures the consequences of their decisions. The fact of good produces the possibility of evil. If there were no relationships, there would be no evil, but because relationships can always be changed, evil is subject to the power of good. We may not comprehend why these conditions should be laid upon us, but as Christians we can take heart that they are not the accidents of an aimless Fate. They are the intentions of a Maker.

Chapter 9

GOD THE FATHER ALMIGHTY, MAKER OF HEAVEN AND EARTH

So far, we have seen the divine Other as the source of natural and human others, all of them indissolubly bound by the processes of exchange into a meaningful pattern. This is an interpretation that modern men clearly can comprehend, whether they are persuaded of its truth or not. When we come to the word "heaven", however, we are faced with an idea that is said by some authorities to be utterly incomprehensible to any modern person. If there be a God, they say, he cannot be apprehended except through the concrete realities of nature and persons, so that to speak of a transcendent God is to refer vacuously to something that is entirely speculative and has no relevance to mankind. And to predicate a supernatural heaven is virtually a return to the three-story universe of primitive superstition.

We have every reason to believe that the authors of the Apostles' Creed did believe in a three-story universe — heaven up there, earth right here, hell down there — although it is doubtful that they were nearly as literal in their interpretation of such words as we accuse them of being. They knew at least as well as we do that if one is going to say anything, he has to say something, and that creatures who normally live in space and time have no choice but to use imagery drawn from spatial and temporal relationships. In fact, it is probable that they were more sophisticated than most of us in their attitude to language, less bound by the letter because of their intensive training in allegory and imagery, and more receptive to the spirit that prompts verbal communication.

Whatever else "heaven" may mean today, the word and concept at least provide a way of referring to our sense that the universe contains more than the immediate, the particular, and the measurable. As words point beyond themselves to the realms of entities and ideas, so entities and ideas sometimes seem to point beyond themselves toward still another realm. The word "tree" is the symbol of a thing. We see the word, and it evokes for us an idea or picture. Seeing an actual tree can be equally èvocative, although it may have on us the same effect as hearing a conversation in a language that we do not know. Evidently the spate of sounds means something, but what it means is hidden from us because we have not learned that language. Many of us occasionally have this perception or feeling or intuition that beyond what we see and think lies something which we are not yet able to grasp. The object in our hand appears to contain subtleties which we have not traced. The use of a word in a sentence intimates that it has a wealth of connotations which are obscure to us. Events occur, even quite ordinary events, which emphatically suggest that "reality" is not what we had always supposed it to be, but that it is or points to something else. Not all persons are haunted by such impressions, but enough of them are that the theologian must pay attention to the phenomenon. Therefore he needs a name for it, and the traditional names are transcendence, heaven, and eternity.

Whether or not there is a transcendent God, we do recognize the quality of transcendence. We can explain it by a number of scientific and philosophical postulates. We can be taught to ignore it or to cultivate it for its emotional by-products. We can affirm or deny that transcendence implies supernaturalism: the Beyond may be mysterious either in the sense that differential calculus is a mystery to one who has not studied mathematics, or in the sense of an impenetrably hidden "God behind God". But however we interpret the experience of transcendence, and whatever word we use to denote it, the experience persists even today and is all the more disturbing to modern men because they are told so often and so authoritatively that it is an illusion, an abnormality, a childish survival, a sentimental indulgence, an evasion of reality, or a stupidity, and that they should not have it at all.

The imperious command not to take such intimations seriously will have several interesting consequences for those who obey it. They will not examine the nature of the phenomenon; they will not explore its implications; they will not develop its potentialities. As more and more people are persuaded to dismiss it, it will occur less frequently and in less mature forms, and more often in forms that are infantile or depraved. Already there are signs that the recent movements to demolish the heavenly throne of the Almighty are leaving us with only two practical alternatives. We can identify our impressions of transcendence as emotions, and turn Christianity into a crutch or a stimulant for our emotional life. Or we can identify them as intellectual insights, and transform Christianity into a rational science. Either way, we shall conceive of God as something to use, not as someone to serve, and in the end we shall almost certainly develop the same attitude toward nature and our fellow men. Having started by worshipping a God who is diffused throughout mankind, we shall be inclined progressively to limit the kinds of people in whom we locate God until we end by worshipping the deity who dwells within the single fragment of mankind which is our own self. Or we shall so broaden our worship that we are dissipated in an orgy of indiscriminate sentimentality.

It may be a coincidence that the contemporary theologians and artists who most stridently proclaim man's alienation from nature and society, and the utter meaninglessness of all existence, are prone also to deny even the remote possibility of a transcendent context for the natural and social worlds. It may also be merely coincidental that those who concentrate their efforts on immediate ends such as social reform are so dangerously tempted to reach those ends immediately that they tend to become ruthless and imperceptive, and to destroy more than they create. While the Christian tradition has insisted that, by the mercy of God, evil is self-abortive, we know so little about the relationships of ideas to one another and to behavior that we must not be hasty in concluding that the results of suppressing our intimations of transcendence are necessarily unfortunate. All the same, the evidence is suggestive enough to justify our re-examining the alternative offered by the doctrine of a transcendent God.

Within traditional Christianity, the belief in an authentically transcendent God serves to keep our eyes turned to the world outside our own selves, which then becomes a counterweight to prevent us from placing disproportionate emphasis upon our inner lives. Conversely, the Christian belief in the authentic reality of the self and nature serves to correct the opposite tendency to annihilate ourselves and others in the transcendence. Historically, Christians have not consistently maintained their balance, but always after a season at one extreme, the inner dynamic of their faith has impelled them either to correct the imbalance, or to break away from Christianity altogether. Because the divine Other created the world, the world must not be scorned or hated. Because man has a history, he must not neglect the intimations of transcendence that occur in history. Heaven and earth are opposite but inseparable, and each is to be known through the other.

The doctrine of transcendence is part of the background for the Christian doctrine of incarnation, which T. S. Eliot has called "the hint half guessed, the gift half understood":[7] the interpenetration of the immanent and the transcendent, history and eternity, body and spirit. Like form and content in poetry, or position and velocity in physics, they can be considered separately, but they do not exist in separation, and it is in their interplay that they are known and fulfilled. The flesh does not become fully itself until it is informed by the spirit. The spirit is ineffectual until it is embodied in flesh — action or word or thing. But even at the height of their union, they do not become identical. Like a man and woman at the climax of sexual intercourse, their difference is heightened in their exchange of felicity. Therefore it is natural that in Christianity the worship of a transcendent God should lead to the foundation of schools and hospitals and to crusades against private and public evils, just as our passionate love for the world should drive us to praise the God who transcends his creation. Back and forth we move between the transcendent Other and the immediate others, neither dividing nor confusing them, but proclaiming their co-inherence.

A NOTE ON "GOOD" AND "LOVE"

WHAT A DEFINITION OR DESCRIPTION OR CREED LEAVES OUT CAN BE as revealing as what it includes. The Apostles' Creed contains neither the word "good" nor the word "love", which seems to me very strange, since the logical connections between the Creed's "God the Father Almighty, Maker of heaven and earth" on the one hand, and our frequent assertions "God is good" and "God is love" on the other, are appallingly weak.

We cannot take refuge in the supposition that the idea of God necessarily implies goodness and love, because history records the worship of several deities whom even their most devout disciples believed to be evil, and because religions of this kind were well known in Christendom at the time the Apostles' Creed was written. Neither can we explain these omissions by saying that everyone who knew anything at all about the Christian faith was already familiar with the belief that God is good and loving. If his goodness and love were so well known as not to need statement, there was no need to mention God at all in the formula, since his existence, omnipotence, and fatherhood were equally obvious.

The only explanation that makes sense to me is that "good" and "love" have to do with values, but that the Creed is not concerned with values at all. It specifies that certain definite and concrete things have happened in the past; certain equally definite and concrete things are happening in the present; and presumably they will continue to happen in the future. It says that the Christian believes in — has faith in, trusts — the assertion that these events did happen. It does not say, "These facts are good," but only "They are facts" — or more precisely, "The Christian believes they are facts". Conceivably, it is no more meaningful or relevant for the Christian to speak of God's goodness than for the scientist to affirm the goodness of the Heisenberg

86

Principle or the chemical composition of sea water. Likewise, to say that God loves may be a legitimate inference from the things he does, but what he does is apparent, and why he does them is not.

Christian theology can be interpreted without reference to goodness and love, and here, such a handling of the material would have the advantage of focusing attention upon the structure of the Creed and its movement from concept to concept. I have concluded, however, that the resulting gain in clarity is outweighed by a concomitant loss in depth, breadth, and height of reference. The Christian understanding of goodness has already been introduced through the back door; here I propose to consider the Christian understanding of love.

All interpretations of Christian love must take account of two facts. First, according to the biblical records, Jesus commanded his followers to love. Second, our emotions are not subject to our will; they are not under our direct control. Because the second point is crucial and is frequently a stumbling block, it will be well to examine it with some care.

As a preliminary, let us take the emotion of anger. We can control our expressions of anger by a direct decision — going for a long walk instead of throwing the furniture around, or throwing furniture instead of beating somebody up. We can sublimate our anger — writing a play or novel with an angry theme instead of indulging in a violent physical attack. We can shift its focus from an innocent bystander to the person guilty of the offense that enraged us. We can feed its flames by constantly reminding ourselves of the original provocation, or grimly turn our attention to something else. We can repress our anger, refusing to express it at all or even denying that we are really angry, although psychologists and psychiatrists have shown that emotions are not destroyed by these methods and that we repress them only at our peril. But we cannot eradicate our anger simply by commanding ourselves to stop being angry, and we cannot generate anger on order, by a fiat of the will making ourselves indignant about something to which we are completely indifferent.

Any real control of anger, or of any other emotion, must be

indirect. An eloquent speaker can persuade his audience that an issue to which they were previously indifferent is actually momentous for them, and work upon their latent emotions to increase their intensity. He can make his hearers comprehend that an injustice is being done, and then stimulate the indignation against injustice which they already possess. Or he can assuage their anger by convincing them that the situation about which they were angry is not what they had believed it to be. Emotions are regulated indirectly by altering the framework within which they occur — a process facilitated by the fact that violent emotions are naturally short-lived, and can be kept at a high pitch over a long period only by devoted nursing.

If, when Jesus commanded his disciples to love, he meant by love an emotion, he was commanding something that is impossible, or inherently destructive, or attainable only by circuitous methods, and therefore he need not be taken very seriously. The alternative is to postulate that he meant by love something which does lie under our immediate control and which therefore is not intrinsically emotional.

The four relationships which we customarily include under the name "love" — affection, deep friendship, sexual love, and *agape* or Christian love — have in common one element that is wholly subject to man's volition: the willingness to exchange, the openness to giving and receiving. The manner of exchange will vary with the type of love and with uncounted factors of individuality and situation. In all love, however, the practice of exchange is cultivated in some style and degree, as in all indifference and scorn and hatred there is resistance to exchange. We have already seen the acts of exchange as necessary and holy. In love, we reach the culmination of exchange: the indescribable fulfilment of man under the lordship of the God who created exchange as our rule of life and commands it as our joy.

Love as exchange can be practised steadily, under all circumstances, without pretending to emotions we do not feel and without disguising from ourselves our spontaneous and honest emotional responses. When we know love as the readiness to give and receive, and practice love by giving and receiving, we are no longer the slaves of our unruly likes and dislikes, but neither are we tyrants over our emotions. Instead, we become capable of exercising our proper authority over that in ourselves which we can directly control: intellect, intention, and action. So doing, we liberate our emotions from a responsibility for direction which they are incapable of handling wisely, and from a despotism which violates their nature. When brought into their rightful place, emotions give power to the firm but chilly structure of intellect and will, adding the warmth of fire without its destructiveness, splendor of color without tawdriness, and a passion that is neither brutal nor timid.

"Thou shalt love the Lord thy God": we are commanded to open ourselves to all he gives and to give him all that we have and are. We are to be willing to exchange in whatever ways he opens to us, and to practise exchange in all that we do, whether by enduring unfathomable abysses of suffering or submitting to the impact of exaltation, by performing heroic deeds or sternly hanging on through boredom or playing like a child at recess from school, or by ascetic intellectual detachment or profound personal involvement.

"Thou shalt love thy neighbor as thyself": and how should we love ourselves? Should we blanket ourselves with tender affection? Should we take ourselves for granted? Should we dislike or disapprove of ourselves? One thing is certain: the Christian should not love himself with his whole heart or mind or soul or strength, because that intensity of love is reserved for the divine Other. For the Christian, there is only one reason for loving self, neighbor, or anything else: because God loves it. There is only one way of loving: the exchange that is our necessity and our blessing. And there is only one fruit of love: the infinite power and variety of interrelationships that together constitute, here and now, the goodness and the love of God.

PART THREE:
THE CRUCIAL PROBLEM

And in Jesus Christ his only Son, our Lord, who was conceived by the Holy Ghost, born of the Virgin Mary, suffered under Pontius Pilate, was crucified, dead, and buried. He descended into hell. The third day he rose again from the dead. He ascended into heaven, and sitteth on the right hand of God the Father Almighty. From thence he shall come to judge the quick and the dead.

Chapter 10

AND IN JESUS CHRIST HIS
ONLY SON, OUR LORD

ACCORDING TO THE TRADITIONAL PUNCTUATION AND PARAGRAPHING
of the English translation of the Apostles' Creed, this phrase
marks the beginning of a new paragraph, but not of a new
sentence. Likewise, in following the sense of the Creed, we
meet here a new problem, but one which cannot be separated
from the preceding discussion without perverting both sections.

I doubt if any aspect of the Christian faith has been so
disastrously affected by the failure to relate the answer to
the appropriate question as the doctrine that Jesus was both
God and man. Therefore it is imperative to spell out the
question which that doctrine purports to answer. The obvious
question is "Who was Jesus the Christ?"—but this cannot be
adequately answered without asking another question, "What
is God supposed to have done in and by Jesus?" This refers
to a still more basic problem, "What needed and needs to be
done?" which in its turn is one phase of the question that is
the key to this entire paragraph, "What is man?"

We can best start from human experience, from the deep
and almost universal human feeling that something is wrong
in our relationships with the world, each other, and ourselves.
It arises in nearly every individual, and in every society of
which we have record. It appears in all known periods of
history. We are uncomfortable somewhere in our deepest being.
We are dissatisfied with practically everything we do. We are
anxious and afraid, but we cannot discover an adequate reason
for our anxiety and fear because when we rid ourselves of one
occasion for them, our distress returns. We feel somehow lost
or alienated from the world, or as if something were radically

out of key, or as if something were missing. We are haunted by a sense of disorientation, the knowledge of death, the dread of meaninglessness. At times we may manage to escape our uneasiness, but usually when we do, we still sense that it is lurking in the background as if waiting to engulf us again.

Every important religious teacher has described, diagnosed, and attempted to cure this uneasiness, dis-ease, disease. Here the differences and likenesses among religions become most apparent, and here they most poignantly bear upon the lives of their adherents. I shall sketch only four of the best-known diagnoses and treatments, in order to make clear what Christianity is rejecting in its doctrine of man and salvation.

Individuality is sometimes identified as the root of man's distress, and the proposed cure is to be the annihilation of his unique personal self in an Absolute where his separate identity will be lost as a drop of water in the ocean or melted as breath into the wind.

The association of spirit with body has often been blamed for these ills. The remedy prescribed for it is the freeing of spirit from body in death, or the ascetic subjugation of the body until — to the degree that is possible — physical needs and pleasures lose their power to affect the spirit and mind.

Ignorance has been singled out as the primary cause of man's disease, with education, further research, new discoveries or insights, or sometimes the mastery over esoteric powers, as supplying new treatments.

Inadequate or corrupt environments are frequently accused of bearing the major blame for man's difficulties, and the solution proposed consists of social transformation, the eradication of poverty and war, the fulfilment of justice, and other such measures.

Christianity, however, declares that our basic problem is sin, which cannot be identified with any of these other states, and cannot be healed by any action or decision of our own.

It is imperative to note that the word is not "sins" but "sin", and sin is not murder or malice or lust or pride or greed, whether as actions or as states of mind. Sin is the condition of the person in which he is at variance with himself or nature or God, or all three. The effects of this condition can be seen everywhere. We are driven by impulses that conflict with one another — toward involvement and detachment, justice and partiality, generosity and avarice, self-preservation and self-sacrifice. We are beset by both nightmares and visions. We are sick with double-mindedness, yet our single-mindedness can turn into a hideous fanaticism. When we search our highest motives, we find them tinged with corruption. When we look at the results of our most noble actions, we find that they have produced unexpected and terrible evil.

There are a thousand ways of describing the state of man in sin. We are by nature bent and need to be straightened. Or we are divided and need to be made whole. Or we are wounded and need healing. Or more simply, we are not what we want to be and obscurely sense that we can and ought to be. But we cannot straighten or heal ourselves, or create integrity in ourselves, because we have nothing to work with except our sick and disintegrated selves. And since all our fellows share that inherent disability, no other human being can do for us what we cannot do for ourselves. The physician cannot heal himself, and he reinfects his patients when he approaches them.

Traditionally, the source of sin has been defined in images taken from the Old Testament: men have desired to be "as gods, knowing good and evil". Frequently the emphasis has been placed on the ethical phrase, "knowing good and evil", but this is a modifier for "Ye shall be as gods", which is by far the more significant. Our most widespread and persistent temptation is to usurp God's place and function in the universe. We want to make ourselves gods by creating worlds for ourselves according to our own specifications. We want to deify our own notions of truth, our own opinions about good and evil, our own dreams of progress. We want everyone else to be just like ourselves. Searching for a superhuman perfection, we bend our divided wills to direct our divided selves in ambiguously good works. Yet this is *our* effort toward *our* ends and by *our* methods, so that *we* remain at the center of initiative, activity, and purpose.

95

Christianity declares that no one is free from this self-assertive and idolatrous impulse. It is expressed in the baby's insistent demand for food, comfort, and attention, in the child's demand to have his own way, in the adolescent's demand for independence, and in the adult's ambitions, however masked under politeness or rationalized as an instinct for self-preservation or lauded as devotion to the general welfare of the human race. Do we seek knowledge, wisdom, peace? Do we work for our children's future? Do we devote our lives to serving our fellow men or our God? These activities are good; they may be holy. But except in the saints, and perhaps even there, they are all tinged with the desire to make ourselves gods.

This is the Christian doctrine of original sin, which does not say that all man's motives and deeds are utterly depraved, but only that none is perfectly good. Some are very far from perfect goodness, some close as a hairsbreadth to it, but none is utterly perfect without spot or stain. The phrases "conceived in sin" and "born in sin" refer to this characteristic of man, and mean simply and only that it is not possible to identify the moment in man's development when he acquires the capacity for or quality of sin, any more than the moment can be identified when an embryo of *homo sapiens* becomes human. Man "inherits" sin as he inherits humanity: the egg and sperm of *homo sapiens* are human cells before they unite to form a new human being.

Theologians differ as to whether the individual is or is not in any real sense guilty for having original sin. They agree, of course, regarding guilt for actual sins — actions (thoughts, desires, choices, behavior) that are contrary to the wholeness for which he was made and which he so urgently craves. Sins are not properly defined by alluding solely to motives or ethical principles; rather, they are violations of the interrelationships that God ordained for creating, sustaining, and developing life. They are offenses against reality. Again the analogy with natural processes is illuminating. Ignorance of gravitation does not protect a baby from hurt when it falls out of its high chair. Neither does ignorance of God's will protect man from the consequences of sin. And the analogy can be carried further.

Knowledge of gravitation or of the will of God does not in itself save one from the effects of carelessness, clumsiness, or deliberate infraction of his principles or commands.

Most Christian theologians say that the gravest consequences for the individual follow from his deliberate sins, the conscious choice of what he knows — or ought to know — is evil, in contrast to sins committed in ignorance or on impulse. He who deliberately resolves to commit an evil act degenerates more than he who errs while trying to do the right thing. In fact, the latter may represent increase of grace: "A condition which of declension would indicate a devil, may of growth indicate a saint."[8] But the effects of the sinful act are not limited by the intention of the actor. They follow inexorably from the nature of the act itself. A cow kicks over a lantern, and a city burns to the ground. No doubt the milkmaid sinned when she carelessly set the lantern within reach of the cow, or when she left her task until it was so dark that she needed a lantern — minor sins, in either case. The total result, however, was the consequence not merely of negligence or sloth, but of the character of fire. Or to reverse the balance of intention and consequence, a self-styled sorcerer can try to destroy the world with a word but fail to harm the fly on the window sill. The effects of sinning upon the individual, and the effects of the sin upon the world, are not to be confused.

So much for the distinction between original sin, the disease which afflicts man, and actual sins, which are symptoms and products of the disease. This, for the Christian, is the central problem of life: not ignorance, not environment and upbringing, not individuality, not imprisonment of spirit in flesh, but sin, which cannot be avoided and cannot be cured by any human effort or treatment.

We are left with two clear possibilities. Either sin is completely incurable, in which case our situation contains no shred of an ultimate hope, and life is and will always remain a dance of festive despair on the brink of nothingness, on earth and beyond earth if there be any such life. Or else the cure for sin comes from outside man. This is the Christian faith and the source of the Christian hope: that our Creator and Lord can save us from our sin.

There are in general three ways by which an omnipotent God could heal us. With a wave of his hand, so to speak, he could override our divided wills, minds, bodies, and hearts. If he did, however, he would destroy our freedom and turn us into slaves or puppets. The cure would annihilate our humanity.

Or God could prescribe for us a course of action, promulgate a set of rules, which when followed would result in a cure. Many people believe that this is what he has done, and all that he has done, but at best it is a partial measure because its success depends upon what man can do by means of his own efforts. For example, when a man tries to become good, he attempts to place his evil impulses under the domination of his good ones. He rejects one part of himself. Such a rejection does not, however, destroy the evil part. It only prevents the direct expression of the evil. Thus the man remains a divided creature, and if anything, he is more deeply divided than before. Repression of this kind can make one into a more pleasant, efficient, and even happy person, at least for a time, but it does not make him whole.

Therefore, Christianity says, God took a third way in which our sin is not amputated as by surgery, or forced into line as by a brace, but is healed as by medicine. The following analogy should not be pressed too far, but it will serve my immediate purpose. As animals are inoculated with certain viruses in order to develop antibodies that can be made into vaccines, so God voluntarily contracted man's disease of sin, knowing that only he could produce antibodies that would be effective against the disease, and knowing also that the process would require him to suffer the agony and death that result from sin. He had to be fully man so that the disease could infect him. He had to be fully God so that he could develop the antibodies for our healing. Only by receiving this vaccine could men be cured without being irremediably maimed in the process. It is as simple and as fundamental as that.

With this as a background, it becomes obvious why Christians have traditionally been so insistent that Jesus the Christ was at once God and man, and why they have so vigorously denied that his manhood was an illusion, as if he wore his flesh like a garment to be put on or taken off as he chose (the docetist heresy), or that God picked a likely lad and infused him with divine qualities (the adoptionist heresy), or that Jesus was an ordinary human being with a genius for spiritual discernment and teaching (the heresy now called humanism). If he be God and not man, he is representing and expounding a life possible only for a god; his death fails to plumb the abysses of our deaths; and his treatment results in crippling our humanity rather than fulfilling it. If he be man and not God, he cannot do the necessary work of introducing the cure into the world, and the job cannot be accomplished at all.

Thus it is necessary for our sakes, for our salvation, that Jesus be fully God and fully man, and without him we are doomed now and forever to a living death of futility and meaninglessness. This is the innermost core of the Christian doctrine of man, that man cannot save himself from sin, but that God can and does save anyone who desires such salvation. And the innermost core of the Christian life — although not by any means always the first event chronologically — is the meeting between human persons and the person who is the incarnation of God.

This meeting has been talked about in terms which make it sound extremely obscure or difficult or private, and with good reason. Most of our direct personal experiences are hard to describe, harder to analyze, and impossible to communicate straightforwardly in the language of philosophy or science. I shall add to the literature on the subject only two short comments. We learn about Jesus in the same ways that we learn about any other person whom we do not know face to face: through persons who did know him, or who have studied his life and the time and place he lived. If we want to find out about Aristotle or Winston Churchill, we read what he wrote; we read what his contemporaries have to say about him; and we consider what scholars have concluded concerning him. Our records of Jesus contain nothing that he wrote, and little by people who directly knew him, but there is that little and it provides a beginning. And though the primary sources — the

Gospels — are brief, the secondary sources in history, archaeology, linguistics, comparative religions, and other relevant disciplines are vast in scope and number.

In learning about Jesus, as in learning about other controversial persons and events, sooner or later we shall reach a point where we must make up our minds on where we, individually and personally, shall stand in relation to him. Was Churchill a hero or a cheap politician? Was Aristotle a misguided enthusiast or the wisest of all men or merely a bore? We may not have to make up our minds about these particular people. They can remain on the fringes of our attention. But when we confront Jesus, our situation becomes almost identical with that of a girl who has received a proposal of marriage. The circumstances compel us to make a decision. We must move from formal belief (the girl accepts or rejects the proposal) to real belief (she marries or does not marry this man). Once the proposal has been made, an answer must be given. Once it has been spoken and heard, neither the lover's "Will you marry me?" nor Jesus' "Will you follow me?" can be evaded. As Gregory Vlastos has written, "There are a thousand ways of saying no; one way of saying yes; and no way of saying anything else."[9] To refuse to answer is an answer. To put off answering is an answer. So is the sudden, surprised recognition that we have already crossed the line between "no" and "yes", in either direction, without realizing at the time that the movement was implied by some other decision. And, of course, to answer forthrightly is to answer.

The circumstances in which the question of Jesus, "Will you follow me?" is asked and answered will vary at least as much as the circumstances in which lovers propose marriage and their beloveds reply. The consequences of the answer are equally unpredictable, whether it be yes or no. Nobody who is entering or refusing marriage knows accurately or extensively what he or she is getting into. Neither does anyone who accepts or rejects Jesus as his Lord. Much of what has been written about "the leap of faith" gives the impression that this is an unprecedented act. Certainly no other choice is as momentous, according to Christian thought. It is unique in degree. But it is common in kind. We do not know what we are getting into when we do anything at all — marrying, writing or receiving a letter, eating dinner, going to bed. They are all leaps in the dark. And no decision, no action, guarantees present or future immunity from pain and error, or fulfilment of our dearest desires.

One more feature of the analogy should be noted. As in our culture the man usually takes the initiative in proposing marriage, so in all times and places God in Christ takes the initiative in approaching his creatures. We respond to God's approach; we do not take the lead. It is not our doing that we have even heard of Jesus. He is known today because God sent him, and because a long succession of men and women have kept alive the story of his life. Moreover, we do not even initiate our own search for God. It is he who, by his Holy Spirit, wakes in us the impulse to seek him, and we could not discover him at all if he had not chosen to reveal himself to his creatures. And once we have made our first tentative response to his summons, we do not find him because we are searching for him, but because he discloses himself to us, either as we become capable of discerning him or as he chooses to waken us.

Everything else in Christian life stems from the meeting where the Son of God asks a person, "Will you follow me?" and the person replies, "I will". That confrontation underlies the Christian's conviction that it is possible for him to be healed, that it is God who has met him on the way, that Jesus is fully God and fully man, and that the world has meaning and purpose and a universal order. Even the recognition of the uncertainty of human knowledge develops out of the encounter where one takes as his basis for action, his faith, the realization that he is met and can be healed: it undercuts his pride, and so teaches him intellectual as well as personal humility. This is what Christianity is all about. This is the Good News, the gospel of Jesus Christ our Lord.

After we have chosen to serve this Lord, we shall learn to recognize his voice when we hear it. God in Christ does not pre-empt authority over those who have chosen other lords: even an earthly ruler would not presume to command subjects of another king. He does not speak with authority except to those who have already acknowledged his authority over them. If he did, he would subvert their freedom.

It is an arduous process, bringing the whole of oneself under God's authority, as marriage is arduous. At first, in either situation, there may be a fine, careless rapture with all of ourselves that we are aware of submitting gladly to the new conditions of life. But life — or God — has a way of dredging up and dumping upon us forgotten pieces of ourselves, unconscious tendencies, unnoticed presuppositions. Each, as it appears, must be placed under authority, and while we can very well decide in advance that we will do so, the actual doing remains a lifelong task. As we submit, and to the extent that we submit, God heals. As we cease trying to make ourselves the sort of persons we want to become, or think we ought to become, he changes us into what we were created to be and shows us the vocations that we were created to perform. But he acts as our guide only as we give him permission. He speaks with us only as we agree, however provisionally or hesitantly, to listen.

Here begins redemption, the work of God by which he brings good out of evil. When we give our divided selves into his hands, he joins the fragments into a new creature in whom nothing is lost, but all is changed by its reorganization. The stones in our nature that we had rejected, he turns into cornerstones of our consummation and his glory. The wasted years become occasions for rejoicing when we use them as periods of preparation. Our remaining sins become opportunities for our oblation and the exercise of his love. Not in themselves good, they are converted into instruments for the creation of good. Like exchange, redemption occurs on natural levels, but is not restricted to them. It can also be holy, a deliberate bringing of sin and sinning creatures to God for him to redirect and, in so doing, convert them and us from evil into good, and from natural goodness into transcendent holiness.

Every age, every culture, every person has a different language and expresses in different forms the breach between man and God, and the means for healing that breach. St. Paul says, "The good that I would, I do not." Dante describes himself as lost in a dark wood, unable to go either forward or back. The patient in psychotherapy says, "I react compulsively." Contemporary existentialists talk of alienation. Nothing testifies more clearly to the timelessness of the Christian gospel than the intimacy with which it speaks to every time and place and person. It is as germane to the age of anxiety as it is to the ages of science, reason, renaissance, revolution, and reformation.

Our hearts are restless, alienated, anxious. We may ascribe our alienation to any circumstance of environment or disposition we choose. They are the occasions for the disease, not its cause. Our anxiety may be temporarily annoying or permanently disabling, but the prominence of the symptoms is not a safe guide to the severity of the disease. This is the fact: our hearts are restless, or they are dead.

It is widely believed that our situation is inevitable, an inherent peculiarity of man, a belief which Christianity shares. It is also widely believed to be irremediable, which Christianity denies. This restlessness is a form of despair, and despair is curable — although because it has its special advantages, we may not want to be cured. Despair enables us to avoid responsibility. It secures us from change. In some respects it is indeed better to live with fixed and invulnerable death-in-life than with the ambiguous chances of hope, the harrowing vicissitudes of duty and disappointment, and the shifts between assurance and uncertainty in our feelings. But Christian hope is not a mood that comes and goes. It is a virtue, a deliberate response to life that we can practise or leave to decay in idleness. It is the Christian belief that our restless hearts can have rest in God. We have ample evidence for it, but it has not been conclusively proved. Every substitute that I know of, however, for the God of Christianity, has failed to provide what Christianity claims to give. Other religions offer other gifts and answer other questions, but we who desire the healing promised by God in Christ Jesus have our hope in him, or we have none at all.

Chapter 11

WHO WAS CONCEIVED BY THE HOLY GHOST, BORN OF THE VIRGIN MARY

THE PROCESS OF CHRISTIAN DEVELOPMENT IS SOMETIMES GRAVELY retarded by failure to see how the parts of the doctrine of Christ are related to the whole. We suppose that we must believe the details before we can believe in the general thesis. We assume, for example, that we cannot believe in Jesus as the Son of God until after we have embraced the doctrine of the Virgin Birth. But this is not the historical sequence by which we received the doctrine. The Christians of the early church first believed that Jesus had healed them and given them a new life, and because of that primal, primary conviction they were ready to believe that there must have been something extraordinary about his origins and his relation to God. We do not know the exact source of the proposal that he was utterly unique — not merely a distinct individual of exceptional power but so remarkable that the only title his followers felt appropriate for him was "the Son of God". But there did come a time when they called him that, and they declared him to be God's only Son because their experience convinced them that he had fully accomplished all that needed to be done. Since his work did not need to be done again or to be supplemented, his place in the economy of creation was that of the Son, not a son, of God. Then they went on to ask what sonship meant in connection with the Son who was at once fully human and fully divine.

A human child is directly derived from his father and mother. Two strains of inheritance are fused in him. At the same time, he is indirectly derived from the God who made us male and female, and decreed that children should partake of the genetic heritage from both their parents. But in the single instance of

104

Jesus, said the early believers, God acted directly instead of indirectly in conceiving his only Son. The Holy Spirit who is God took the place of a human father. For a special purpose, God employed a special method, not departing from his general process of derivation but short-circuiting it, as any of us may normally delegate a task to someone else but on one occasion do it with our own hands. The direct derivation of Jesus from God can be interpreted as violating natural law if those laws are interpreted as meaning impersonal, autonomous mechanisms. If, on the contrary, natural laws are understood as exhibiting God's faithfulness to his creation, they are derived from him and are subject to him, and for him to depart from his customary procedures is not to be unfaithful but to exercise his power in another way.

But the word "unique" must not be applied to Jesus without qualification. While traditional Christianity has insisted that he was uniquely the Son of God, it denies that he was uniquely human, and the Apostles' Creed pounds at his humanity in phrase after phrase: "born of the Virgin Mary, suffered under Pontius Pilate, was crucified, dead, and buried." The child was said to have been fathered directly by God, and mothered by a human woman who sprang from human parents, and they from theirs, and so on. Why should Christians care whether his mother was a virgin? Some do not; others deny it. The tradition of Mary's virginity, however, guards a valid point, because if she were sexually experienced, it might be concluded that her son Jesus was no more than human, and if this were true, then we would not have the hope that is communicated in the Son of God.

Overemphasis on Mary's virginity can lead to a dangerous underemphasis upon one of the most striking and important implications of Mary's motherhood: that the body is not — as Gnostics and other "spiritualizers" have claimed from the beginning until now — evil in itself, or insignificant, or antagonistic to the holiness of God. Rather its physical, material, anatomical, and physiological realities are compatible with deity itself. Matter may be a lower form of existence than spirit (although the difference in kind does not require us to

105

assume a difference in value) but it is not hostile to spirit. Had it been, God could not have become flesh and dwelt among us. And if the body is capable of holiness, then the functions necessary for its continuance, its productiveness, and even its pleasure are good and may become holy. We degrade the creation as well as the incarnation when we become so engrossed in the question of Mary's sexual life or the way in which her Son was conceived that we overlook the obvious point of the biblical stories themselves: her absolute physical, as well as mental and spiritual, obedience to what God asked of her, and his authority over her body as well as over her spirit and mind.

The doctrine of the Virgin Birth guards still another concept that is even more important than Mary's virginity or her obedience: the doctrine of history which is implied by her motherhood. Jesus is said to be neither an entirely foreign body introduced forcibly into history and nature, nor entirely the product of historical processes and natural selection. Our salvation is neither an imposition upon us from outside nor a natural progression within us. But in the person of his Son, the very God who rules and sustains nature became a part of nature. The creator of history entered history as a historical person. He subjected himself to the laws and conditions that he had created. It is quite possible that this entry of God into nature and history can be stated in words and images more acceptable to modern ears than the Virgin Birth, but the alternatives that have come to my attention are even less satisfactory than the ancient formula. The phrases "conceived by the Holy Ghost, born of the Virgin Mary" make unequivocally clear the belief that at every stage of his incarnation Jesus was at once God and man. He did not acquire deity after he became man, nor was his humanity in any way or at any time a pretense. It is down to earth as he was man, up to heaven as he was God, and so it preserves for us the hope of salvation.

Chapter 12

SUFFERED UNDER PONTIUS PILATE, WAS CRUCIFIED, DEAD, AND BURIED

THE REFERENCE TO THE ROMAN GOVERNOR NAILS DOWN THE EVENTS to a specific time in history, as "suffered . . . dead, and buried" nail them down to nature through the lives of all creatures who have suffered and died, and whose bodies have been disposed of by one means or another. He suffered.

The cross itself, as used during the reign of Tiberius, consisted of an upright stake called a STIPES — which was generally fixed permanently in a cement socket at the place of execution — and a cross-beam called a PATIBULUM, a baulk of timber about seven or eight feet long which the victim was compelled, as part of the punishment, to shoulder from the prison-store to the waiting upright. A notch, or some other similar wood-joint, close to the top of this upright, allowed the cross-beam to be nailed or bolted in position, and about four or five feet from the ground there would be a series of holes to allow the insertion of a peg, called SEDILIS EXCESSUS, to support the victim's crotch: this was to prevent the entire weight of the body from slowly dragging the hands and arms from the nails or other fixing.

After the scourging the victim would be cut down, kicked and dragged to his feet, and, carrying the PATIBULUM, would be driven on by blows from the flat of the sword, or goaded with it, to the place of execution.

And there the victim would be felled to the ground, the PATIBULUM would be thrust beneath his neck, his arms gripped and then tied to the cross-beam with cords, and his hands nailed to it with heavy iron nails, square in section. This nailing would be either through the palm or the forward fold of the wrist, and was intended to prevent the hands jerking free during the convulsions which crucifixion produced.

Then the cross-beam would be dragged across the ground to the STIPES and hoisted up until it could be secured in the notch. Other cords might be tied around the waist as an added precaution against the convulsions of agony jerking the body even off the nails — in would go the supporting peg — and then, finally, the feet themselves would be nailed, either with one nail driven between the metatarsal bones of the two crossed insteps, or with two nails, one through each heel behind the Achilles tendon.

And there he remained hanging until he died, anything up to seven, eight, or nine days later.

... This was a death of movement, ceaseless movement, ceaseless writhing and twisting, seeking for some relief, some lesser pain, some temporary stay on death, some lull in the onslaught on the senses, an easement which cannot be found, for there is none...[10]

He suffered. He by whom all things were made permitted these atrocities to be perpetrated against himself. He suffered as other men, innocent and guilty, have suffered. He died as other men have died: alone, in agony, and ignorant of what might follow death.

Men had desired to be as gods. They had sought for untold centuries to take God's place in the universe and to be themselves the masters of their fates and the captains of their souls. In crucifying Jesus, they followed that desire and decision to its extreme limit. Trying to displace God, they tortured and killed him.

It has been pointed out that Jesus' judges and executioners did not believe him to be God. They did not know what they were doing. They did not mean to. But the offense that in law is called criminal negligence has intellectual and spiritual counterparts. Jesus' enemies did not, so far as we know, think their position through. But they had every opportunity and capacity for doing so. As Jesus implied when he spoke from the cross, they needed forgiveness precisely because they could and ought to have known what they were doing. They can be excused for not knowing that he was God: even his disciples seem not to have been sure of it then. But they ought to have known that he was speaking to their condition. They had ears but refused to hear. They had eyes but did not look. "By no jugglings of fate, by no unforeseeable coincidence, by no supernatural machinations, but by that destiny which is character, and by the unimaginative following of their ordinary standards of behaviour, they were led, with a ghastly inevitability, to the commission of the crime of crimes."[11]

By suffering from the actions of sinful men, God in Christ involved himself directly with all the sufferings of all the victims of natural processes and of freedom. But he did more than share our griefs and sorrows. He shared our sin. To illustrate: a father gives his son permission to drive the family car and in a moment of carelessness or overconfidence or bad judgement, the boy wrecks it. Obviously the father is not responsible for the accident, but it is equally obvious that he is responsible for allowing his son to use the car. So while the father is not directly guilty, he participates in his son's guilt and shares the responsibility for the damage. Christianity declares that God gave man freedom. Man abused it. And God not only endures the results of that abuse, as the human father pays for repairing or replacing the old car, but also, in his incarnation, God publicly acknowledged his initial responsibility for giving man freedom, and in the crucifixion he acknowledged the justice of his children's cry, "You shouldn't have let me do it!"

God does not stand apart from our sin, or from us in our sin, observing with detachment the mess we have gotten ourselves into. He joins us within our sin. He who is without sin unites himself with us so that even in our fiercest iniquities we are not alone. We are not alone in our protests against the conditions of our existence or in our anguish at being what we are, because he also protested against and agonized in them. Neither are we alone in our exaltations and loves, because he also loved and was exalted. By his incarnation, life, and death he openly demonstrated the unity of God with man. By our response to him, we affirm or deny our unity with him.

He died and was buried. The whole person who was indivisibly body and spirit, God and man, died. We cannot help remembering that he was raised from the dead, so that it is nearly impossible for us to feel the poignancy of his death. We gloss over it in many ways. He only appeared to die. Or his body died but his soul went marching on. Or he knew that God would raise him (and the correct translation is not "he

109

rose" but "he was raised"), so that nobody need pay any particular attention to the event — it was quite like taking an anaesthetic and coming out from under the drug at the appointed time. Any or all of these statements may be true, but none of them represents the Christian faith. Christianity asserts that the person Jesus the Christ, the only Son of God, really, entirely, and unambiguously died. How important this is will be seen only when we discuss the resurrection and the forgiveness of sins.

Before leaving this chapter, I want to call attention to the Creed's silence regarding the teachings of Jesus. None of the classic creeds — Apostles', Nicene, or Athanasian — say a single word about what Jesus taught or mentions that he was a teacher. They treat that aspect of his life as if it had not occurred. This lacuna, like that regarding "good" and "love", cannot be readily explained on the ground that what was omitted from the formula could safely be taken for granted. It is more plausible to conclude that the writers of these creeds believed the essence of the faith to lie not in what Jesus said, but in who he was and what he did.

In the light of the popular belief that Jesus was and is significant primarily for his ethical teachings, it is worth noting that the Creed's assertions are not ethical but theological. Ethics deals with what men do or should do, and theology with the nature of the world, man, and God — the epistemology, metaphysics, and anthropology which provide the groundwork for ethical determinations. The creeds prescribe one and only one action as necessary for the Christian: so deep a trust in God in Christ Jesus that it results in action. It is not difficult to see why trust should be paramount. If we do believe rightly about these matters, we shall spontaneously follow what Jesus taught. If we do not believe rightly, we cannot obey him except in superficial formalities, and no amount of labor or intelligence will enable us to go farther. This is not because the Christian has supernatural assistance, but because if Christianity is in fact true, the Christian is not at odds with reality. And because the Christian — within the degree possible to him — sees the world in the way that Jesus did, he can conform his life to

Jesus' teaching with a delicacy, a swiftness, a suppleness that cannot be imitated and cannot be achieved by even the most meticulous obedience to rules. His inner integrity, and his integration with the world, enable him to act firmly and easily as a whole — not a divided — person.

The argument is often heard that non-Christians live as nobly, or more nobly, than Christians, even by explicitly Christian standards. So long as the faith is understood as a state rather than a process, and ethically rather than theologically and personally, this is a decisively destructive criticism because it is true. The Christian ideal of integrity and holiness represents our orientation rather than our accomplishment, even in the best of us. Christians do not have a monopoly on virtue any more than they have a monopoly on exchange and derivation, and it is both dishonest and discourteous to claim that they do or to attribute virtue in non-Christians to some sort of latent Christian tendency. Christians do not even have a monopoly on redemption or salvation. What they do have is the joyous conviction that while goodness may be attainable through God known by other means, it is attainable through God known in Christ, and that while a person may be healed of his sin by God working through Christ in ways other than those of Christianity, he can be healed through the knowledge and love which Christianity offers him.

Christianity categorically denies that man can heal himself. Christians should not assert that God's power to heal is the exclusive property of the church or the faithful, because that would deny the doctrine of his omnipotence. The difference between "may" and "can" is perhaps hair-splitting, but it is no more abstruse than the difference in a housewife's attitude toward a tried and an untried cake recipe. She knows by experience that the one will turn out well; the other may or may not. The theological names for these two categories are "covenanted" and "uncovenanted". God may disclose himself and give his gifts in any manner at all, but he has promised to be with those who call upon his Son.

But divine promises are likely to contain a divine catch. He will indeed come when we call, but he will come in the way

111

that he chooses, which may not be the way that we expect or want or have prayed for. We ask his guidance and support for our enterprises, and he may reply by destroying them. We beg his blessing, and may receive a condemnation which is all the more severe because we had invoked him selfishly or proudly. We petition him for our daily bread, and may be stupefied to receive a banquet. By inviting his presence, we open ourselves to the incalculable.

The value to us of Jesus' teaching is not, in the last analysis, that it tells us what to do or how to do it, but that it mediates a world view and a quality of life against which we can measure our own. Our records of what Jesus taught are scattered, sometimes contradictory on the surface, and directed to situations that are conspicuously different from our own. But when we test ourselves against what is there, we are ashamed. We try to obey his teachings on wealth and marriage and the Kingdom of God, and we fail. And then we obstinately go on. We seek beyond the specific instructions for their source; and we find a particular view of the world, a particular understanding of reality; and we find a person. Then we come back from that vision and encounter seeing our old world with new eyes, living a new kind of life that grows not from acquiring new ideas but from confronting a person who renews us.

Chapter 13

HE DESCENDED INTO HELL

ANY ALLUSION TO HELL IN SERIOUS DISCOURSE IS LIKELY TO BE A stumbling block, and a great many Christians welcome the ways to avoid it when it appears in the Apostles' Creed. They note that it is probably a late addition to the Creed, which gives them a good, scholarly reason for leaving it out of consideration. Or they interpret it as a figure of speech meaning no more than that Jesus experienced every mode and degree of existence that man is subject to. Or they define it as the place of the dead rather than a condition of punishment. Or they recall the desire for vengeance that produces the primitive idea of retribution, and conclude by treating the concept as nonsense, or as a superstition which they are fortunate or wise enough to have outgrown.

But the tradition, however unbiblical, that defines hell as the place or state of the damned, by no means arises from guilt or vindictiveness alone. It illuminates one of the most important problems associated with the Christian belief in human freedom. By traditional definition, heaven is God's presence known as a joy and a fulfilment, and hell is either the impression that God is absent, or his presence experienced as a torment. If man has any freedom, then he must be free not only to seek God and to co-inhere with him, but also to seek and associate with something other than God. Or if we prefer a more neutral set of images, he is free to choose between reality and illusion. Here and in any hereafter, we can love or hate, learn or close our minds, live in exchange or isolation, and the final question is not whether our definition of reality or God is correct, but whether we are open to correction.

Beneath the medieval imagery and the corruptions of Christian teaching that hamper our consideration of hell, lies its basic definition as a condition rather than a place, and not so much a punishment inflicted upon persons who were mistaken in their theological and ethical judgements, as the inevitable consequences of their desiring to live in a way that is hellish. With Milton's Satan, the damned would rather reign in hell than serve in heaven. And the rest of us are not much better. We grumble at injustice instead of redeeming or forgiving it. We cling to attitudes that cannot be justified by evidence, intelligence, or love. We excuse our pride by calling it self-respect, and our self-centeredness by calling it self-preservation. We place our comfort before our responsibilities, and rationalize our laziness, anger, envy, malice, and ambition until we see them as virtues. In fear of ridicule, we license the cynic and the scoffer when they blacken our faith and our motives for believing it. Being divided within ourselves, we are attracted to hell as well as to heaven. Dante showed himself to be a most penetrating student of humanity, as well as a discerning theologian, when he portrayed the damned as pushing and shoving in their hurry to reach their appointed circles in hell. They will be tortured infinitely and interminably, and they know it, but now they can have their own way forever, and that is what they most deeply desire.

So stated, the choice between heaven and hell sounds obvious if not easy, but those who have taken the decision seriously know otherwise. In fact, it is the desperate choice between crucifixion and alienation. Tradition says that Jesus endured both. Having suffered crucifixion — heaven's method of redemption — he suffered also the alienation of those who during their natural lifetimes chose unreality, either because they did not know any alternative or because hell was what they wanted. And he took to that depth of changeless negation the possibility of an alteration. Some theologians believe that this opportunity lies always before the inhabitants of hell, in this life or in any other there may be. Those in hell who decide to leave can do so at any time, but no one is compelled to. The only restriction for entering heaven is the willingness to live in heaven's way: to receive and to give, to love and to learn, and to rejoice in the dependence of all things upon the Father and Maker and Lover of them all. If we do not want to exchange and love and be dependent, we are in hell although we have entered through pearly gates and are walking streets of gold and have taken up residence in one of the mansions of the City of God, because we hate the glory that surrounds us and despise the joys that are given us there. If we do want what heaven has to give, we are citizens already of that City.

In the end, therefore, the interpretation of hell as eternal pain is a proclamation of the triumph of God's love: that his victory is complete even over those of his creatures who refuse his love. Love makes us free; love unimaginably sustains us in our freedom not to love. A God who loved us less would wrest our freedom from us to save us in spite of ourselves, or withdraw from us his blinding presence and thrust us into nothingness. But the God of Christianity *loves*. He loves even those who hate him. And he loves them not only in what they might become, but in what they are, and in his love he upholds their right and capacity to repudiate love. This is love's victory, that he loves without return, as the exchange of love is the celebration of his victory.

Chapter 14

THE THIRD DAY HE ROSE
AGAIN FROM THE DEAD

BOTH AS A UNIQUE HISTORICAL EVENT AND AS AN INSTANCE OF THE
general class "resurrections", the raising of Jesus from the dead
is so conspicuous that it becomes the extreme example, and
meets the fate of most such extremes. One group of interpreters
dissevers it from history and nature by stressing its uniqueness
or by defining it as a "spiritual" event discernible only by the
eye of faith. Another group, anxious to certify its affinity with
history and nature, ends by denying that anything significant
occurred.

It is reasonable to reject Jesus' resurrection and the general
resurrection on the ground that we have no coercive evidence
for their historical authenticity. But neither do we have such
evidence to the contrary. All that we have is, on one hand, a
denial based upon the fact that we did not observe the incident
and upon the theoretical incompatibility of the whole notion
of resurrection with certain beliefs about history and natural
law. On the other hand we have an affirmation based upon reports from people who conceivably may have been fully as accurate in their observations and reports as we imagine ourselves
to be, and upon another belief about history and natural law.
We cannot separate our beliefs about the resurrection, pro or
con, from our comprehensive views of knowledge and the world.

Some idea of the complexity of the problem can be indi-
cated by a series of questions. Are historical events to be ac-
counted real and not legendary only if they agree with our
ideas about nature? Or should we test the validity of natural
laws by our observations of historical events? To take an illustration from another setting: shall our attitude toward the

fire-walkers of India be determined by what contemporary Western scientists tell us about the invariable effects of fire on the human body? Or shall we modify our teaching and study of burns to bring them into line with our observations of fire-walking? The choice might seem self-evident, particularly since fire-walking, like the resurrection, can be "scientifically" explained by what we presume to be the psychological states of the participants and observers. But is this adequate? Are natural laws merely convenient summaries of historical events, including laboratory experiments, so that the final arbiter is history? Or are historical events merely individual instances within an eternally stable pattern of interlocking natural laws, so that the final standard is nature, and anything that contravenes what we know — or believe we know — about nature is therefore to be understood as an illusion?

We can legitimately judge Jesus' resurrection by the criteria of science, although if we do, we shall be duty-bound to judge every other event that purports to be historical — like the evolution of mind from inorganic chemicals — by the same criteria. If the resurrection is to be discarded on the ground that it could not have been predicted and cannot be repeated, the same must be said of evolution. If we do not trust the emotional balance and intelligence of those who claimed to see Jesus die and live again, we shall be hard put to justify our trust in the emotional balance and intelligence of commentators who know the event only by hearsay. Or we can judge science by the standard of the resurrection, and declare that a science which does not allow for this occurrence is incomplete, and a science that categorically repudiates it is defective.

To borrow a distinction from C. S. Lewis, when we of this scientific age contemplate the stars, we are prone to see "the army of unalterable law" where our forebears saw "the revelry of insatiable love".[12] In one way these two visions are coherent with each other because personal love can express itself through inexorable routines. But in another way they are utterly incoherent, because impersonal forces cannot love or rejoice. As Christians, we can confidently trust science when it tells us about the army of unalterable law. Where we go wrong is in

117

letting ourselves be browbeaten by those scientists and others who insist that law excludes revelry, and that we are not permitted to believe in some things, like the resurrection, because they are not compatible with an impersonal, mechanically structured view of nature.

These comments on science have been a necessary digression — necessary in order to indicate that we do not have to wait for authorization from science before we can allow ourselves to take the resurrection as an article of faith, and a digression because it has nothing to do with the positive reasons why so many Christians have not only believed that the doctrine is true, but have staked their lives on the belief in it. Essentially, the doctrine answers the question, "Do we live in a world where the tree lies as it fell, where the past is beyond redemption, where the Omnipotence can be defeated?" Certainly this is the world of the crucifixion, and by and large the world of our daily lives. In it, evil overcomes good and man overcomes God, not in appearance only but in dreadful fact. The child has died and cannot be restored to life. We have sinned and the effects of our sin will persist forever. Youth is gone and we shall never get it back. The ultimate outrage has happened; we knew that it could not, but it has. But the doctrine of the resurrection says of them all: they are not lost; they will be restored; they can be redeemed.

The world of the resurrection includes the world of the crucifixion. We are in bondage to nature, but nature itself is in bondage to God. We are victims of the past, but the God who created history is competent to use even the past for his own ends. When we die, the dead past is not left behind us, but goes with us into the process by which we are perfected. Jesus' resurrection is our warrant that though we die with our healing and our work incomplete, they will be completed, and though our fathers' sins are visited upon us and ours upon our children, these sins can be redeemed both within time and beyond time. The evil of the past is one of the factors that created the present; therefore it endures in the present, and being present, it can be corrected here. Nature is not merely the stage on which we act, and history not merely a drama in which we are actors for a scene or two. They are the means by which all things are made available to the healing power of God, means of grace by which we become exposed to the operation of the glory.

When Jesus was raised from the dead, he was changed so radically and so compellingly that the portions of the Gospels describing his return have in their style, as well as their content, a note of unreality. He was manifesting a new life, not an enhanced form of his old life. Even more strikingly, he was exhibiting a new world whose difference from our ordinary world is most effectively demonstrated by the difference it made in those who saw it through him. They did not only change their manner of living or their direction or goal or their ideas about the world. They seem to have become in a substantial sense "new men".

Few experiences have such a forcible impact upon us as that when the world turns upside down in front of us, and we discover that it is not simply better or worse than we had anticipated, but is fundamentally different in all its relationships and possibilities and principles of organization. Often in this experience there is little sense that we have changed; only instead of being at home in a familiar but heightened world, we now live in a strange country where we cannot recognize the landmarks, and we do not know what its dangers or sanctuaries are, or where are its boundaries. The new world may be so foreign to the old that what we had thought were unbreakable laws of nature are now seen to be habits of thought that can readily be changed. Self-evident truths cease to be self-evident and their truth is questioned. And "possible" and "impossible", "valuable" and "worthless" may change their settled places.

That experience, or something very like it, seems to have happened to the disciples at Jesus' resurrection, and happens to their successors when they grasp the meaning of the resurrection and believe in it. More broadly, it happens in religious and antireligious conversions, which may be startling events occurring in a moment, or so slow that we do not realize what has occurred until we look back and see how once we were religious or antagonistic to religion, and now are not. Time and

119

again, the change within ourselves is the product of a change in what we understand the world to be. The psychological alteration follows a transformation in our world view. We see a new world, and then we become new creatures.

The three days between Jesus' death and resurrection are not critically important for theology, since what is at stake theologically is the nature of the universe rather than the duration of an event. Nature and history are both subject to the God who raised his Son from the dead. He does not rescind his laws or undo the past, but he provides a way for them to bring us within his redemptive process. The God who created us will, in his own time and way, recreate all that he has made — except the things that refuse his redemption, and even they, unwittingly and unwillingly, shall disclose his glory and love.

Chapter 15

HE ASCENDED INTO HEAVEN

JESUS' ASCENSION CONCLUDED AND SUMMARIZED HIS LIFE ON EARTH.
Like his conception, birth, ministry, death, and resurrection, it
is grossly physical and therefore an affront to the multitudes for
whom the material world is an inferior or evil form of existence.
(It was Evelyn Underhill who wrote, "I am gradually finding
out that most devout persons are docetists without knowing it,
and that nothing short of complete unreality will satisfy
them."[13]) Traditionally, Christian theologians have said that
this final act was no mere "spiritual uplift", but a lifting up of
the flesh that was the incarnation of the whole person. Fully man
he lived, died, and was raised. Fully man he ascended into
heaven. Salvation was brought to us by means of matter, and
salvation encompasses matter. We are redeemed with and
through the material world, not from it.

The first and most critical question about Jesus' ascension is,
"What did God do here?" And for once, the most obvious
answer is also the most profound. His life in nature and history
had an end as well as a beginning. What needed to be done had
been fully accomplished. We do not need to wait for his next
lecture or another of his confrontations with religious and secular
authorities, in which he will explain in more detail what he has
already said or add further information about what we need to
do. His incarnation had been designed for the purpose of healing man's disease, and now that the cure was available, he did
not have to stay around to apply it himself. His work here had
ended, and it was imperative to manifest first that it was indeed
completed, and second that the remedy was equally available to
everyone. Direct communication with him in face-to-face encounters, and the unmediated touch of the divine-human hand,

121

did not convey special graces or confer special privileges. The opportunity to participate in his life, that had originally been limited to a few first-century Palestinians, was being granted to all.

The conclusion of Jesus' ministry as a Jew in Palestine does not imply the end of his ministry to men, but instead, that he is equally effective — and equally efficient — in his ministry whether he acts indirectly through our neighbors or directly by becoming a neighbor in a small community in the Near East. He is with all men and every man, and he functions in both ways. Whether any person shall be with or against him shall depend upon that person's own choice, and not upon historical or natural accidents. The ascension of Jesus, terminating one phase and form of his activity among men, is the sign of his universal presence and the guarantee that he is accessible to everyone everywhere who calls upon him.

A second answer to the question, "What did God do here?" extends and deepens the first. When Jesus became incarnate, he received our flesh and our heritage of nature and history. When he ascended, he took them with him into the very Godhead, so that our human nature is not only represented symbolically in the divine nature but is substantially present there. God is in us, and we are in him. By Jesus' ascent to our common Father, we are united in all ways of interchange with the ultimate, awful Other.

Therefore Jesus is with us and we in him, not solely as a memory but as a continuing actual presence, and not as he might impose himself upon nature and history but as he operates powerfully within them. His energy toward our redemption can be facilitated or impeded. The potentiality of grace is not automatically realized, and probably is never made completely real without something analogous to crucifixion. But by means of his ascension, our world has been taken into God and is therefore intrinsically sacramental, and any life may become a sacrament. Any piece of bread can communicate a divine as well as a natural sustenance. Any event can be an act of consecration. None must be. We are not passive victims of an inexorable progress toward salvation, nor is the divine grace so uniformly diffused through the world that we can say "All is God" or "God is All" with the pantheists. Instead, we are penetrated by a life that is not our own, that we do not acquire by working for it, and that we do not deserve. It is given to us because we are loved.

This, in substance, is what has been called the sacramental view of the world: that it is infused with a holiness which is explicitly realized — made real — in the sacraments of the church. Thus baptism and holy communion do more than excite memory, or stimulate imagination, or signify a covenant. They actually convey the holy to man. At the same time, they do not introduce an alien substance into human affairs, because the holiness of God is everywhere. In the sacraments, however, the grace that is usually hidden is made plain, and the power that is latent everywhere is actively released upon the participants. This has always been possible, but before the incarnation, the sacramental life meant primarily the descent of God upon man. Now that single, simple movement has been completed by another, the lifting up of our manhood into God. In one way we are already there, by virtue of the ascension. The gift has already been given. But we have not already accepted it for ourselves, much less lifted other persons and things into him by those prayers which are offerings rather than intercessions, where we present the world to him with the utmost desire that his will may be done in it, as it is in heaven.

Between the beginning of this chapter and its end, the question has changed from "What did God do?" to "What is God doing?" — an alteration which reflects the experience of many Christians that the life precedes the faith. They are not lifted up with their Lord because they believe in his ascension; but because he has lifted them, they believe and believe in the doctrine.

Chapter 16

AND SITTETH ON THE RIGHT HAND OF GOD THE FATHER ALMIGHTY

"OF COURSE GOD DOES NOT HAVE HANDS. OR A LONG WHITE BEARD. He does not sit on a throne, with Jesus on a slightly lower and smaller throne beside him. Of course God is not really what we mean by a 'person' at all. But neither is he the ghostly kind of being that we think of when we say 'a spirit'. He is not male or female, or an asexual being, or a thing. He cannot be perceived by eyes or ears or touch, or be comprehended by the mind. He is not in any place or all places, and he is somehow in, but also outside of, time."

Such negatives are valuable as means of expressing the proper modesty of finite creatures in confronting the infinite. We can, however, become overanxious in using them, and so tightly circumscribe our talk about God with qualifications that we destroy in ourselves and others any sense of the reality to which we are referring. We become so fearful of being wrong that we end by having nothing to be wrong about. Only an extremely robust communion with God can survive this kind of attack on our imagery, and times without number we have ruthlessly quenched the first glimmerings of the holy by scrupulously insisting on precise or complete statements. But as C. S. Lewis wrote with reference to literary criticism:

> To take a man up very sharp, to demand sternly that he shall explain himself, to dodge to and fro with your questions, to pounce on every apparent inconsistency, may be a good way of exposing a false witness or a malingerer. Unfortunately, it is also the way of making sure that if a shy or tongue-tied man has a true and difficult tale to tell you will never learn it. The armed and suspicious approach which may save you from being bamboozled by a bad author may also blind and deafen you

124

to the shy and elusive merits — especially if they are unfashionable — of a good one.[14]

Systematic negation can be as dogmatic as systematic affirmation, and is as prevalent among the devoutly religious as among atheists. "You must not think of God as an old man with a long white beard. He is a spirit." But the image of the patriarch may arouse our love and worship, and the image or rejection of imagery implied by "spirit" may do nothing except confuse us. The figure of the old man is not adequate for a fully developed Christian theology, but it can be entirely appropriate and even essential at some stages in the development of the Christian life, and useful at any stage for the expression of certain functions or values — and not as a false image to be outgrown, but as a priceless insight to be assimilated. In rejecting the image of God as a venerable old man, we are likely to lose the idea which the image signifies. In refusing all imagery, we deprive ourselves of the means to correct and enlarge our understanding of what lies behind every image of the divine.

Another peril lurks in identifying "the right hand of God" as only an image, a figure of speech and thought. While certainly this is both true and important, many of us are severely tempted to label anything in Christianity that we dislike or disagree with as a figure of speech, and then we feel free to dismiss it from consideration or construe it in any way that will satisfy our current prejudices. If, however, Christianity is true while we are not yet wholly in the truth, we can expect some aspects of the faith to be obscure to our unenlightened minds and repugnant to our unsanctified tastes. "Let no man be hasty to eat of the fruits of paradise before his time," wrote Jeremy Taylor.[15] We do not grow into the great truths overnight, and the process — like physical maturation — cannot safely be rushed. Being novices in the faith, we probably do not like or agree with everything in Christian doctrine and practice, and there is no merit in pretending to ourselves or others that we do. Neither is there any merit in accepting blindly such doctrines as we do not understand. But we do well when we return occasionally to reflect upon concepts that previously seemed foolish to us, like that of God's having hands, in case we may now be ready to see a little sense in them.

125

Perhaps the notion that God has hands is no more out of the way than the notion that Jesus laid his hands upon the sick, or our notion that the hands of our own beloved, touching ours, communicate a blessing.

Having dealt with these preliminaries, we can approach the theological meaning of this clause. To sit at the right hand of a person is to have the place of honor, and implicitly to recognize degrees of honor. It is tacitly to affirm the existence of a structure of authority and obedience — virtues that can be difficult to understand and even more difficult to practise in a society that first interprets democracy as egalitarianism, and then deifies it.

"I'm as good as you are." Christianity has insisted through the centuries that there is truth in this assertion. As Father and Son are equal in their deity, so created things are equal in their creaturehood. Confronting God, man cannot claim essential superiority over sparrows or stones, or inferiority to insects or tornadoes, because they — like him — are created by God. Much less can we appropriately exalt the educated mind over the educated heart, or intuition over logic, or one man over any other man. With respect to their creaturehood, there is equality between Shakespeare and the latest popular poetaster, Einstein and the dabbler in witchcraft, athlete and invalid, saint and sinner. At the same time, however, the hierarchy of ability and achievement is inescapable. Being individual creatures, we are different from one another. Being different, some of us are inferior and others superior in particular functions like writing poetry, exploring nature, repairing automobiles, and preparing meals. In general, we are consistently better at some things and worse at others. But the status of such functions with respect to one another is constantly changing, so that superiority or inferiority in a given activity does not convey an absolute position, but is always determined by its relation to a specific purpose.

Few of us find it easy to live serenely with either our authority or our subordination, or our powers or weaknesses, even when they are conspicuous. "I'm better than you are at doing this" is usually considered an offensive remark, and "You're better at it than I am" is nearly as objectionable. As a rule we cannot accept degrees of ability or authority in ourselves or others as the matters of fact that they are, calling for neither vainglory nor chagrin but for simple acceptance. Yet those of us who have been blessed by studying under great teachers, or who have watched an experienced craftsman at his work, will recall the incomparable delight of looking up to a master — one of the purest and most innocent pleasures that life gives us. Another is its opposite: to know our own competence for the task at hand, that we are masters of a tool, a process, an idea.

Most of our difficulties with the simple acceptance of hierarchies in function proceed from our failure to relate the concepts of hierarchy and equality in the proper way. Without the foundation of equality in essential being, authority is oppressive and obedience is shameful. Only when teacher and student, parent and child, employer and employee, administrator and subordinate, mutually affirm their intrinsic equality do they become free to exercise their rightful power without tyranny, and to serve without becoming servile.

To insist on the distinction between equality in creaturehood and hierarchy in function is another example of the hair-splitting whose consequences are intensely practical. Between equal beings there can be no envy or condescension. Between different beings there must be discrimination. Only those who are equal can fully exchange without risk of destruction; only those who are different can exchange at all. By dividing essence and function, the unity of creation and the diversity of created things can be maintained without contradiction. We can thus admit our limitations without resentment and use our capacities without restraint, because our equality does not depend upon what we have in the way of gifts or how we use them, but upon our status as creatures of God. If we repudiate the functions for which he has designed us, whether low or exalted, or if we perform them badly because we resent his will for us, or if in the interests of "democracy" we deify equality and debase hierarchy, we are still his creatures, and as much his as are those who welcome and fulfil their functions. It is our loss when we desert our position and our work. It is our gain when we accept the place and vocation for which we were created.

In traditional Christian theology, the prototype of equality in

127

existence and hierarchy in function is said to be the Godhead. The Son does not displace the Father, nor is he incorporated into the Father. He sits at his Father's right hand, equal to God in his deity yet inferior to God in his manhood, utterly obedient to God yet in authority over everything created by God. The Father and the Son are one, and therefore equal. They are different, and therefore they function hierarchically. The pattern of relationships that characterizes the holy and glorious Trinity is repeated in the household and the state, among men, and between men and God. It remains for us to use and enjoy it.

Chapter 17

FROM THENCE HE SHALL COME TO JUDGE THE QUICK AND THE DEAD

IS THERE NO END TO OUR PERPLEXITY, OUR STRUGGLE, OUR HUNGER? Must we always approach but never attain the fullness of grace and love? Christianity says that there is an end to the world's pain and our own, and a satisfaction of its longing and ours, because all things are moving not toward cessation but toward consummation. As individuals we shall die. Our societies will disintegrate. Nature and history will cease. But that does not conclude the matter. There is to be a reckoning. When it will finally happen, and how, we do not know any more than we know when nature and history began. Meanwhile, we live under the continuing judgement of the same Other who will judge us in the end: the God who has taken humanity into the Godhead, Jesus Christ our Lord.

He not only was, but is, man. He knows by experience what we endure, so we can trust him to understand us. He is God and knows the purpose for which we are made, so we can trust him to be righteous — and right. Often we may have wished that we knew someone who really understood us, and we do. We live *sub specie aeternitatis,* within a light that dissolves the fog of our pretensions and that penetrates our bones, disclosing in a flash the division between what we believe ourselves to be, and what we are. As Charles Morgan says in his play *The River Line,* a man may let us off if we implore, "Please, I didn't know! Please, I didn't mean it!" But: "go to Nature and say, 'I didn't understand! I didn't intend!' Nature will flick you away like a dead fly. ... You can't cry off. You have to bear responsibility for the wrong that came through you."[16] And God is more, not less, just than nature. We can be forgiven, but we are not excused.

129

At our best, we do not want to be excused. If our failures can be explained away by blaming our heredity or environment or present pressures, so can our successes. If this outburst of rage or that surrender to lust is attributed to a physiological condition, then we were not responsible, and not to be responsible is not to be fully a person. At our best we would rather be openly wrong than written off as negligible playthings of natural processes or history or fate. But we are not always at our best, and we feel that to be ashamed is to write ourselves off — not as things unworthy of notice, but as deserving condemnation. Before God, we are nothing or we are ashamed, and the Christian tradition declares that we are guilty and ought to be ashamed, but still we are something and not nothing. We are responsible beings who no doubt have abused their freedom and made dishonest as well as honest mistakes; we are worthy perhaps of damnation but worth the attention of the omnipotent God. By judging us, he asserts that we are important to him, and thereby he confirms our hope, as well as our fear, that our lives are significant both to him and to the world.

The Christian doctrine of final judgement, therefore, contains the decisive affirmation that our lives have a finite conclusion but an infinite importance, so that even after our world ends, its existence and ours are justified. In addition, the doctrine says that justice shall be fulfilled among men, and between man and God. The sins committed against us and the sins we have committed shall be paid for by repentance or by alienation, whichever we prefer. Our fellows are answerable to us and we to them. And the God who accuses us has submitted himself to our accusation. We have ample grounds for denouncing him. Theology and art, particularly, spell out our charges against our creator. He has set us impossible tasks under intolerable conditions. He has allowed love to become a torment and grace a searing whip. He has not cut down the transgressor or eased the way of the faithful. Charles Williams points to Jesus' "incredible comment on Judas — 'it were good for that man if he had not been born' ". And then Williams asks, "And who caused him to be born?"[17] So we put God on trial, sentence him to torture and death, and duly execute him. Justice is fulfilled: he has paid for what he has done.

130

And we shall pay for what we have done. He requires of us no more than he requires of himself.

All through our lives, we anticipate the final judgement in those moments of insight when we see what form our lives are taking, and compare it with what its form should be — or what we envision that it should be. For the Christian, both the actuality and the vision are subject to judgement by the norm of human nature, the incarnate Son of God. But often we take some other norm. We erect standards that are not appropriate for us, or perhaps for any human being, and try to make ourselves impassive as stones, or pure as angels, or righteous as God himself. Or we judge our thoughts, motives, and behavior by external standards that have nothing to do with the person who is in the process of being formed, and without considering whether the standard is appropriate to one who is at that stage on his journey. In Christianity — perhaps always but certainly today — the discipline of self-examination and the sacrament of confession involve more than release from guilt. Their present function is primarily twofold: to restore and clarify our sense of the form our lives are taking, by admitting those betrayals that hold us captive to our past; and being absolved of them, to see with a new simplicity, a new innocence, the form our lives should take in our relationships with others and the Other. Burdened by consciousness of sin, we cannot look outward to others and the Other, yet until we meet them face to face, we cannot know who we are or should be.

The encounter with God where we open ourselves to his judgement is supremely a meeting of persons. Most of us, however, are badly prepared for it because we have allowed the depersonalized detachment and fragmentation that are prerequisites for certain limited purposes, to operate in areas of living that are intrinsically personal. We accept more or less without question governmental control by agencies whose official representatives function anonymously. In nearly all fields, the pronouncement, "That's only your personal opinion" is given and taken as a reproach, as if to be a person were incompatible with, or destructive of, valid perception. Students are graded for their cerebral competence in dealing with objective data, and scholars

131

are judged in great part by their capacity to exclude from their deliberations any flavor that could be labelled "subjective bias" — or wisdom. We have been systematically transforming persons into things, and then wondering why our mental hospitals are crowded. Starvation of the person is as definite a disease as starvation of body or mind or emotions, and since the person is central to all, it is far more difficult to treat than other starvations, and its effects are far more damaging to man and society. We are incapacitated for living and dying, for resurrection and for that judgement where the issue is "Who are you?" Then we cannot hide behind good intentions or deeds or thoughts. Then we know ourselves as we are known: either as impersonal things that are repelled by God as some insects are repelled by light, or as persons who spring toward him and are perfected in their individual and personal glory.

PART FOUR:
THE CONSUMMATION

I believe in the Holy Ghost, the Holy Catholic Church, the Communion of Saints, the forgiveness of sins, the resurrection of the body, and the life everlasting. Amen.

Chapter 18

I BELIEVE IN THE HOLY GHOST

THE DOCTRINE OF THE HOLY SPIRIT IS THE MOST ELUSIVE OF ALL Christian teachings because it is he who gives us the power to perceive and respond to God. Therefore the attempt to identify the Holy Spirit closely resembles the attempt to observe, with our own eyes, our own seeing apparatus. We see by means of the eye, the ocular nerve, and the brain, but in seeing we do not perceive the instruments of sight. They perform their functions because they conceal themselves, and we know of their presence by the fact that we see, not by directly watching them in action.

Consequently, the nature of the Holy Spirit must be approached indirectly. Probably the most fruitful way is through the doctrine of the Holy Trinity, by which Christianity affirms that God is one but denies that he is solitary. This concept was not developed solely to resolve a logical contradiction, or to correlate scattered biblical passages, and certainly not to indulge the appetite for subtle argument. In essence, it expresses the Christian's assurance that God in Christ Jesus is both a *God* to whom we can pray, and a God to whom we can *pray*:[18] one who is simultaneously wholly other and wholly accessible to us. That he is wholly accessible, Christians have known from what Jesus did in healing them. That he is wholly other, they know through their sense of living under a transcendent judgement. But how can he be at once so near and so far? How can we meet him in the world and still know him to be infinitely beyond the world? The Trinitarian solution is not only a masterpiece of analysis that answers a question in logic, but also it is a passionate fusion of separate strands in our actual living, a response to our desperate need for integrity and to our almost equally desperate need for a way by which we can speak of these matters.

135

No description of the Holy Trinity will be fully adequate. The one that follows is to me clearer than any other.

From its Hebrew heritage, Christianity has derived the belief that only God is God, and that he is one and indivisible. He expresses himself by creating and sustaining the world. His hand can be seen at work in natural and human events, and his love in his covenant with his people. The Christian experience of Jesus has led to the further conviction that God determined to show himself to men not only indirectly and partially through nature and history, but directly and fully. His Son is his complete and perfect self-expression: his own Word by which he discloses to us who and what he is, his own Name for himself in relation to us. However, God did not first exist, and then express or name himself. His existence is inseparable from its expression. At the same time, the expressive Name — like an artist's work — has its own existence independently of its source. Thus God's Name for himself, the Word that openly declares him to humanity, is at once the fullness of his being and a being distinct from himself. By the incarnation of Jesus the Christ, God uttered this word aloud to his human creatures. Jesus is fully God and yet different from God, and between them there is perfect exchange, perfect love.

Another strand of experience, the awareness of the immediate power of God working upon and through his creation, engenders the doctrine of the Holy Spirit. He is the Power and Gift and Grace of the first two persons of the Trinity. They did not first exist, however, and then exercise their power to bestow their grace. By the very fact of existing, they send forth blessing, they radiate love, and they supply the energy for all other blessings and loves. Our own capacity to know and love God, and our desire to grow in his grace and truth, are not ours by natural right or inherent aptitude, but by the gift of the Holy Spirit. These gifts may be unrecognized as his, or may be refused or wrongly identified or misused. Or they may be apprehended and adored in his own person — because the Power and Gift and Glory are traditionally understood not as an energy like electricity, or as an ability like conscience, or as a radiance like the mystical vision, but as a person — in the words of the Nicene

136

Creed, "the Lord and Giver of life". So some early representations of the Trinity show the Godhead as three men: all alike, all young, sitting together at a table on which there is bread and wine.

By means of that image, and the experiences and concepts that underlie the image, we can begin to understand why Christians have not been content with a solitary God, but have maintained that he is "one God in Trinity, and Trinity in Unity", and why they have predicated three persons rather than two or a dozen.

If we define love as willing exchange, then a solitary God cannot love because he has nothing apart from himself with which to enter an adequate exchange — an exchange adequate to his capacity. By creating a world, he could indeed provide himself with something to love and be loved by, but not on a basis that could conceivably establish a consummate interchange. The disproportion between Creator and creation is too great, and a solitary God could not come down from heaven to institute proportion. A God who has nothing except his creatures to love remains essentially solitary. Further, if God depends upon us for love, then upon our shoulders is placed the burden of his loneliness. Only we can deliver him from his isolation; he comes to us in his need. But must we pitiful, wavering, empty things sustain our Maker? Are we indispensable to the Omnipotence? Is the Person of Love so starved for love that he must create a world to love and be loved by? The idea is either frivolous or unbearable.

The alternative begins with the presupposition that God possesses already, in his three Persons, the fullness of the exchanges of love in all its degrees of hierarchy and equality, and in all its forms of direct, indirect, and reciprocal derivation. Two persons would not be enough to exhaust the types of exchange; more than three would be redundant. He created his world — or worlds — as an expression of his love and by means of his love. He does not need our love in return, but like human lovers all through the ages, he seeks to include others within the joy of his love. Love is magnanimous by nature. It spreads itself abroad out of its richness, and is not diminished when its gifts are refused. Thus in the Christian understanding, God does not crave

137

our love in order to meet his insufficiency. He desires it for our sake, because only through loving him can we enter the joyous destiny for which we are created and in which we are recreated.

It is humbling to believe that God does not need us for his satisfaction, or even to accomplish his work. Being omnipotent, he does have other hands than our hands, and if he so desires, he can raise out of the stones creatures who will do his will. But having granted that, two other things need to be said. First, he freely loves us enough to die for us, and greater love hath no God than this. Second, his call to us is a call to rejoice, to praise, to come freely because this is our greatest delight, rather than a plea for us to come to his rescue. Thus we are liberated from the duty of bearing God, and liberated into the relief of being borne. Moreover, we can love him without constraint or obligation or responsibility to love. Or we can freely not love, if we prefer the shreds of life in ourselves to the consummation of life in him.

To "grow in the Spirit" is therefore not to undertake a special discipline designed to foster a peculiarly "spiritual" faculty that is ordinarily undeveloped, but instead to sharpen the vision we already have with respect to what we are already doing, until we can recognize the Spirit readily and follow him without stumbling. It should not be supposed, however, that we shall invariably know him at once whenever he appears, because he is as likely to be the skeleton at the feast as the guest of honor. He gives the bread of life and takes away the tainted food which we crave but which would destroy us if we were to eat it. He empowers us to respond to God, and checks our natural tendency to enthrone ourselves beside or above God. We are prone not to welcome the Spirit's leading: like children who protest bitterly when they are not allowed to play in a busy street, counting it proof that their parents do not love them, we inveigh against the Spirit when he obstructs the ambitions which, if attained, would smash us. And when we receive joy, we take it as our due and not as his gift.

The work of the Holy Spirit in resisting man needs to be stressed because as a rule we do not expect to find him in the role of destroyer, and not because he works more often or efficiently in this way than by comforting our sorrows, helping us in our duties, and illuminating our journey. This is not to say that all defeat and suffering are the gifts of God, but only that he works even with them, and his Spirit penetrates them. We cannot be sure, when all things conspire to frustrate our intentions, whether God is using them to redirect us toward himself, or whether other men are opposing God's will for us, or whether there is no God at all. All that we as Christians can properly claim is that by and large we are not responsible for what happens to us, but we are immediately responsible for the way we respond to these happenings, and for the degree to which we prepare ourselves for the critical situations that are likely to arise: for death and judgement, for life and love.

"Thou art a God who hidest thyself," cried Isaiah. The eye does not see itself. The Holy Spirit does not show himself, nor does he always make clear to us the Father or the Son. By hiding himself, by concealing that his activities are his, he ensures that we shall not be overwhelmed by the presence of the holy and omnipotent God. The initiative is always his, and he does not tell us in advance what day or hour he will show himself to us, or under what circumstances he will meet us. Therefore it is incumbent upon us to be continually alert for his appearance in a human face, an event, a perception, a machine, an institution, a dream. Because by every means except coercion, the Holy Spirit labors to bring us to himself, and through himself to the Father and the Son: the Gift, the Glory, and the Name.

Chapter 19

THE HOLY CATHOLIC CHURCH, THE COMMUNION OF SAINTS

THE PHRASES "THE HOLY CATHOLIC CHURCH" AND "THE
Communion of Saints" are ways of stating the Christian's recognition that we do not live or die unto ourselves, but are members one of another. We are made to live in community, and
Christianity is a community before it is a theology or a faith.

Two common misconceptions must be cleared away before
we can examine the Christian community in any detail. Here,
the word "saint" does not refer specifically to persons who have
been or are considered worthy to be officially canonized. In the
context of the Apostles' Creed, it is an inclusive rather than an
exclusive term, embracing all those who have responded deliberately and joyously to the call of God in Christ that they shall
live from and for one another. They may be wise or foolish,
young or old, highly educated or unlettered, and they form a
community not because they intend any such outcome, but because community results inevitably from the manner in which
they live, from exchange.

The second misconception has to do with the word "church",
which we tend to read either too abstractly or too parochially.
Most of us can readily believe in an ideal and preferably invisible church as being a divine community, but we find it almost impossible to believe in the ecclesiastical organization down
the street as being anything more than a human association. Yet
in all traditions, the church is by definition visible and material
and local: an incarnate body existing in space and time, not a
fellowship of disembodied spirits but an actuality like a nation
or a club. The other error is to identify our own exclusive branch
of the Christian tradition as the one and only church, and to feel

140

or even to think that other branches are betraying what we feel is the authentic pattern — the one to which we are devoted. The church is not, however, fundamentally a collection of persons who are joined by a common heritage or intellectual agreement or similar emotions or shared activities, but of persons who are bound together by the acts through which they express their common faithfulness to the Person who loves them.

Man is by nature — which is to say that he is by necessity — a social being. Born dependent, he cannot live unless food and protection are given him during his infancy and childhood. Born human, he cannot become a person except by associating with other persons. And all his life as a person is determined more by his response to the question, "With whom shall I stand?" than by his reply to the inquiry, "What do I know and what shall I believe?" His convictions may determine his loyalties, and his loyalties will certainly influence his convictions: there will be a continuing interplay between them. But loyalty is more basic than knowledge or intellectual conviction because it is more primitive. Knowledge is of the mind and faith of the person, but loyalty is of the blood, of levels that lie far deeper than consciousness and will. Thus the person who is exiled or disowned does not merely suffer from loneliness. His veins are cut. We rarely see the effects of exile, disownment, or excommunication today except in primitive societies, partly because in the more sophisticated cultures our root loyalties are overlaid with so many superficial ones, and partly because so few of us are disowned by our families or sentenced to exile that we do not realize how vitally we depend upon those to whom we are loyal. We do not outgrow this response because it is primitive only in the sense of being primal, a characteristic not of the childhood of mankind but of its elemental nature. We can forsake our families, churches, nations, or whatever, by proclaiming our independence. We can be deprived of our social foundations when a particular community dissolves or its other members die. But these separations are not comparable to the personal catastrophe that follows being cast out, and our ancestors were wiser than we when they feared exile and excommunication nearly as much, or as much, as they feared death.

141

The primordial need to belong in a society affects every phase of our growth, and the shrill or sullen defiance of all social intercourse is pathological. At times any of us may need solitude as a balance to society. At times some of us are impelled to stand against one society in the name and for the sake of another. But the human need for a social ground is imperative, and preferably that ground should transcend immediate, face-to-face social contacts. It should stretch into the far past and future, as well as into all parts of the world. The doctrine of the Communion of Saints is most meaningful for our time when stress is placed upon its being a community extending throughout all space and time, and comprising all those who are called to live by exchange under obedience to God in Christ. Because it exists in all times it is available to every time, and no one is exiled or excluded from it except by his own choice. It does not dissolve, and death does not separate us from it.

C. S. Lewis describes this community when he writes of those

> who willingly accept and honourably and happily maintain that complex system of exchanged services on which society depends. There is nothing to distinguish them from people outside the company except the fact that they do consciously and joyously, and therefore excellently, what everyone save parasites has to do in some fashion. From one point of view they are merely good slaves, good soldiers, good clergy, good counsellors and the like. But their goodness in each vocation springs from the fact that they have taken into their hearts the doctrine of Exchange, have made 'singular and mutual confession' of 'the mansion and session of each in each'. As a result there is, inside the company, no real slavery or real superiority. Slavery there becomes freedom and dominion becomes service. As willed necessity is freedom, so willed hierarchy becomes equality . . .[19]

This description is especially interesting in that by implication it excludes the spurious piety of putting only a part of one's mind on his work, while another part devotes itself to "religious subjects". Some tasks indeed come so close to being automatic that they can be used as opportunities for meditation or prayer, but a mechanic or physician or artist or housewife or anyone who thus divides his mind will almost certainly do his work less well than he can and should, and will end by offering his Lord a slipshod or half-finished product, and by betraying his co-workers. These are forms of sacrilege, offenses against the God who labored in creation and saw that the work itself was good.

Within the Communion of Saints, whose members exchange by choice as well as by necessity, there exists a group which interprets the exchanges sacramentally: the Holy Catholic Church. It has defined only certain forms of exchange as sacraments, but it holds that any act can be sacramental in character if it effectively expresses and conveys the grace of God. Since the entire creation springs from God's love, everything in it can be a means of communion with him, and anything can be consecrated by his power. We do not make it holy. As in all other matters since the beginning of the world, primary initiative lies always with him who enables his creatures to act as well as to respond. We can call upon him. We can present this person or that situation for his blessing. It is he, however, who consecrates them, lifting them into the source from which they came.

Originally and now, the church serves two weighty purposes. First, it witnesses steadily through the vicissitudes of history and spatial distance to the fact that we live from God in Christ, and therefore we live from each other. Prophets come and go. Individual believers die or abandon their faith. Unorganized companies dissolve. But institutions endure — sometimes, it must be conceded, long after they have become ineffective or corrupt. Second, the institution of the church provides a setting in which Christians as a body can openly declare and develop the exchanges of Christian community and, as well, offer their relationships with men and communities outside the church for consecration. The first function of the church requires it to maintain the integrity of the Christian gospel. Its second function requires it to be a body with members, organized in that hierarchy of functions which exposes the essential equality of all created beings. It is not to be an organization with a constituency which does not radically alter if it loses or gains a component, but an organism that suffers throughout and is fulfilled throughout as its members arrive and leave, suffer and grow.

As individuals we can profess our devotion to and derivation from God in Christ, and our interdependence with our fellows.

As Christian individuals we should do so. But to identify individual actions with the action of the church is like identifying "I love you" with "We love each other" — and no one who has ever been in love will ever confuse these statements. By the church's "We love each other", we affirm together a mutual interdependence that frees us from the isolation of independence as well as from the sterility of absorption in an undifferentiated mass. Where each gives life to all the others, none can be superfluous. Where each receives life from all the others, none can be alone. The church, like the human body, supports the uniqueness of each of its members, and their unique gifts sustain its life and effectiveness. They live from it; it lives from them.

This vision of the church loses much of its impressiveness when we look at the churches we know in our own neighborhoods. With tragic persistence, these local institutions degenerate into social clubs, welfare organizations, lecture forums, or concert halls. They cater to the current tastes and interests of their congregations by offering manipulation of moods instead of sacraments, psychotherapeutic counselling instead of the forgiveness of sins, entertainment instead of discipline, and sociability instead of the anguished and glorified body of Christ. Well-publicized, fashionable projects are exalted over day-to-day good workmanship; zealous support of exciting enterprises is substituted for dependable friendliness toward the neighbor whom God has placed at our side; and religiosity takes the place of disciplined worship, the high rigors of sanctity, and intelligent, plodding hard work for the correction of social and personal ills.

Because the Christian life is necessarily a life within a community, there can be no such thing as a solitary Christian. But there are many Christians, as well as inquirers into Christianity, who are repelled by the churches to which they have access. Often they are urged to become active in a parish in order to give it new life, to be the leaven in the dough, and some of them try. That, however, is a job for a reformer, a warrior of the Lord who has a special vocation for the task, and special equipment in the form of tenacious roots fastened deeply into a community that transcends the immediate one. To place such a demand upon those who have quieter temperaments or are called to other vocations is to ask what is both inappropriate and impossible.

I am convinced that there are far more isolated Christians than most church members and leaders suppose. A good many of them retain formal affiliation with a parish church. Some work assiduously in it, distressed though they be by their failure to find in it what they need, by their inability to diagnose the reason for their failure, and by the fear — open or hidden — that the fault lies in their own hardness of heart. It can be that. But also, it can be that they are hungering for food which the local churches ought to supply and do not. Those who profess to be Christian while remaining outside a local congregation are perhaps more shadowed by despair than by self-reproach, but their state is equally wretched.

The position of the isolated Christian is both miserable and dangerous: miserable because of its loneliness and hunger; dangerous because it is only by associating with others that the individual can achieve and preserve a sense of proportion. Detached from exchange with the community of believers, he cannot help but exaggerate whatever meets his individual circumstances, so that his faith becomes an expression of private bias. At the same time, his position is filled with grace and hope when his rejection of the church he sees is founded upon his faithfulness to the church that he does not see.

The discrepancy between the idea of the universal and invisible church, and what goes on in local congregations, not only reflects the sin and sins of men, but also exhibits an important aspect of the incarnation. Matter is not at enmity with spirit. Jesus was not less God because he was man. The parish church is not a degraded form of the universal church but its incarnation, the means by which the universal church participates in nature and history. For this reason, we create difficulties for ourselves when we approach the doctrine of the church by first envisioning an abstract ideal, and then bending every effort to impose that design upon our institutions and ourselves. By so doing, we attempt to force our concept of the divine upon nature and history. We reverse the incarnation, whose method was to grow within them. Instead of beginning with an ideal,

145

we should begin where we are — and where we are is in groups of two or three or a dozen where authentic community already exists, both within particular, concrete institutions and outside them. We have been brought together for any of a thousand purposes and by any of a thousand chances of propinquity, and we have realized at some stage, often with astonishment, that more was happening among us than we had intended. The Spirit of God was moving among us, impregnating our relationship with his power and grace.

Such small, spontaneous groups do not possess the Spirit. He possesses them, although their members may try to coerce him with rituals and organizations, prayers and silences. Neither do they constitute churches. They are instead representatives of a special vocation within the church, and thus they are to the congregations what the prophets are to the priesthood, so that neither is fully adequate without the other. In our communal lives as in our personal lives, we need both stable structures and dynamic movement, but the two functions cannot be performed by the same entities. The formally organized institutional churches must be firm like bone to preserve the identity of Christian history and doctrine, and to supply the resistance that supports and controls motion. The Spirit-filled groups are and should remain fluid like blood, informal and unformed, incessantly changing and instantly responsive — and like blood, they are partly generated by the marrow of the bones.

The necessity of the church is established by the God who made man such that his humanity cannot be fulfilled except as he lives in community, and every Christian congregation is a witness to that fact. No matter how often or how tragically it fails to provide the blessedness of intimate communion, or how harshly it condemns communities of the faith with which it is not in communion, it is still a witness. Its structure is derived from the nature of human nature and history, as Jesus' flesh was derived from his mother's flesh, and the institutions are not — or should not be — ashamed of their lineage. Neither should they be ashamed of their proper function: to provide a durable and dependable social framework that will enable communion to take place as the Spirit gives his gift of continual

146

regeneration by the groups that are especially his. The institutions constitute the enabling structure. They are the Body waiting to be directed by the Spirit. They discipline our spirits by their faithfulness in maintaining their own stable life, and by becoming a center of loyalty for the fervent spontaneous fellowships, a home from which they can journey as they must and to which they can always return.

The institutional churches, at every level of organization, exist for the sake of the informal communities of the Spirit, and the little communities for the sake of the formally organized churches. Each saves the other; neither can save itself. They perform their respective functions, however, only so long as they remain themselves and not when the attempt is made to transform congregations into prophetic or ecstatic bodies, or to stabilize the Spirit-filled groups with a constitution, officers, and rigid definitions of purpose. Sin on both sides has impelled us toward both errors. Local congregations and international denominations are harried by those who would turn the institution into a corps of social reformers or a fellowship of intensely consecrated intimates. And the informal gatherings are petrified by those who would bind them under the direction of a congregation or minister. So we exalt or discredit the spontaneous gatherings as "little churches within the church" composed of a religious élite, even though here, as in the Godhead, "none is afore or after another; none is greater or less than another".[20] The formal congregations and the informal gatherings are equal in existence. In the hierarchy of function, sometimes one and sometimes the other takes precedence as the Spirit determines; and they are equally necessary for the continuing incarnation of the Body of Christ.

Chapter 20

THE FORGIVENESS OF SINS,
THE RESURRECTION OF THE BODY

THE HEART OF THE CHRISTIAN FAITH CONSISTS OF THE ACT OF GOD whereby he saves men, but the exact description of salvation has had to wait for these two phrases. They come almost at the end of the Creed and they comprehend all that has gone before, because salvation is the change from fragmentation into integrity, from sickness into health, from evil into good, and from sin into sanctity. The Apostles' Creed sums this up as the forgiveness of sins, and it makes a special point of including the material world in the process. The phrase "the resurrection of the body" declares that the entire person — body as well as mind, will, emotion, and spirit — and nature as well as history, are caught up in the transformation effected by the forgiveness of sins.

Many of us become confused in thinking about forgiveness because of the deeply rooted belief that forgiving is inextricably associated with forgetting. Especially, we are likely to believe that unless we have forgotten, we have not truly forgiven — or unless those whom we have sinned against have forgotten the wrong, they have not forgiven us. That, however, is not the traditional Christian interpretation of forgiveness. Christianity is more realistic than that. Forgetting is not something we can do on command, so that if forgetting is necessary to forgiving, we have no control over our forgiveness and it would be fatuous to require us, as Christianity does, to forgive sins committed against us. Also, forgetting is ultimately undesirable because it destroys integrity. The sin is a part of us, and to suppress it by forgetting is to split us in two. And in any event, Christian forgiveness is concerned not with the acknowledgement and payment of debts, but with the renewing of persons.

In Christian doctrine, only God has the power to forgive, and our forgiveness of each other is possible only by our participation in his forgiving acts. We can forgive because he forgives. And he does not say to the sinner, "Your sin is forgotten." He does not say, "It does not matter." Neither does he take the sinner back into the relationship they had had before the sin was committed. The past is not abandoned or forgotten and our previous status is not re-established. But what, then, can forgiveness mean? What can it do?

What God says is, in effect, this: "You have sinned, but *even this* sin shall not cut us off from each other. *Even this* shall not cause me to forsake you. You have done wrong, but together we can transform that wrong, bring good out of evil. You have been broken, but with your consent, I will heal you. Your sin does not divide us unless you choose that it shall. Our relationship is so strong that it can survive *even this*."

The penitent replies, in effect: "Neither will I let *even this* cut me off from you. I am yours still. I deserve that you should forsake me, but since you are faithful to me although I have been faithless to you, we shall build again together. Nothing can ever be the same again between us, because I have betrayed you. But I accept your promise that together we can redeem *even this* — and even me. I will not let my sin or my shame divide me from you."

Much of our difficulty in achieving such a reconciliation arises because it is natural that we should want to avoid those whom we have injured. When we face them, we cannot help remembering our offense, and we strongly suspect that they also remember it. The injury and the shame combine like stones and mortar to build walls between those whose relationship contains a sin. In most circumstances, it is relatively easy for us to surmount these barriers when it is we who have been sinned against. Forgiving is a generosity that leaves our self-esteem intact. But the denial of the self in shame is another matter. Yet until we have recognized our act as a sin and accepted ourselves as sinners, we cannot even begin the laborious

149

and exacting work of entering the redemptive process, much less helping to bring the sins of the world to God for his action upon them.

Forgiveness is a mutual covenant, an act of exchange. God pledges that he will not cease from sustaining the sinner. The sinner pledges that he will not allow his sin to prevent him from accepting life from God. The fundamental relationship of giving and receiving shall be recreated. As if to witness to his faithfulness in forgiving, God does not destroy sinners, else we should all be dead — or more probably, have never been born. In the Eden story, God came to man after the Fall as he had before. It was man who avoided God because of his shame.

The fact of the sin inserts a new element into the relationship of God with man and of man with man. The question now and always is whether the element of sin shall determine the character of the entire relationship, or whether the relationship will be strong enough to absorb that element and transmute it to the service of the relationship. God's relationship to man can survive man's sin. He upholds our existence even though we have sinned and keep on sinning and do not repent. But we, like Adam and Eve, are tempted to feel that the one fact of our sin overrides all the other facts in our relationship to God. We do not accept his forgiveness, or forgive him for having permitted us to sin, and therefore we cannot forgive other persons or ourselves.

As Christians — even as human beings — we cannot in honesty deny the facts of our sins and sin. But given these facts, we can declare either that the sin is the most important aspect of our relationships, or that the most important aspect is the power and love of God. We can determine that our sin shall be more powerful than God's love in our relationships with him, or we can turn to him and let him bring *even this* sin into the pattern of interchanged love, as he brought the killing of his Son — of himself — into that pattern.

Forgiveness of man by God, and acceptance by man of God's forgiveness, renews our dependence upon God. Since he refuses to let sin be the defining factor in his relationships with us, we can forgive each other and renew our mutual interdependence with other men. However, this secondary forgiveness between men is more complicated. None of us is free from every shred of sin in any relationship. Our lives are so intertwined that we all share, in some degree, in the sins of others and they in ours. In the very act of forgiving, we need to repent of our own terrible sin.

The renewal of exchange is the necessary preliminary to redemption, the process in which sin is transformed by its inclusion within the pattern of love. Natural redemption goes on all around us, as when a lovers' quarrel ends in reconciliation on a new basis of understanding. The sin — anger — becomes an occasion for a deeper exchange of joy. The fact of the anger is not forgotten or ignored. The sinfulness of the anger is not glossed over. But the sin is used to generate good, and its new function as a source of good places it in a new context, thus giving it a new character. In itself, it was evil. Being a source of good, it is good. It has been converted, turned around, from evil to good. And any sin can be converted by this process except the sin against the Holy Spirit: the sin of blocking the channels through which forgiveness flows, of refusing to accept forgiveness, of holding grudges or clutching onto one's guilt, of cutting oneself off from the changes and exchanges that are the work of the Spirit and his gifts.

One more type of sin needs to be brought explicitly into this picture: the sins we commit against ourselves. The failure to forgive ourselves results inevitably in disintegration, one part of the person repudiating another part. "I did it, but I'm not really that sort of person! ... I did it, and I can't bear to remember it! ... I am doing it, but I loathe myself for it! ... God may forgive me, but I cannot forgive myself!" In such ways do we cling to the belief that forgiveness and redemption are products of our own efforts, and not the work of God. Giving lip service to the doctrine that we are sinners, we are overcome with dismay when we realize that we have committed and are committing sins. Avowing that God can bring good out of any evil, we act as if the Omnipotence is not competent to deal with this sin of ours. Instead of bringing him all that we are that he may use it in his time, in his way, and to his end, we try to dissociate ourselves from our sins in order to parade before him how much we can do.

The alternative is to admit, "I did it, so I am this sort of person. Now I know myself better than I did before — how sick and inadequate I am. I know now how much I need healing and how preposterous it is to think that I can heal myself." Such a confession unites us with ourselves. Then the newly integrated self can go to God and say, "This, in all its ugliness, is what I am. Forgive me. Save me from myself." The formal belief that sins are forgiven becomes real belief, faith, when it is put into action, when we take ourselves to God, and placing ourselves into his hands, turn to the next step of doing whatever he has set before us to do. So long as we are gazing in horror at our sin or cringing away from it, we are not paying enough attention to God that we can find out what his will for us may be. We are not reconciled with ourselves or with him. Only in penitence do we become whole.

The Christian doctrine of salvation embraces not only the forgiveness of sins, but also the resurrection of the body and therefore of the history and nature that are exhibited in the body. It is not only sins that are eligible for redemption, but sinners, and not only the present, but also the future and the past. If it be possible to know a person in his entire meaning without regard to his physical functions or actions or his participation in temporal events, belief in the resurrection of the body is superfluous. Or if we suppose that God gave us flesh as a punishment, or as a temporary discipline, or because he was indifferent to us, or because he permitted an inferior deity to create us, then we can dispense with this doctrine. But if we give God credit for omnipotence and love — and efficiency — we must accept our bodies as being the method he chose for working out his will, and therefore they are not to be thrown aside or transcended but to be cherished and redeemed.

A helpful analogy comes from the work of the artist. When he chooses a medium for his work, be it sounds or paint or words, he is limited by that medium, but without it he could do nothing at all. Since the medium is at once the means of his expression and the restraint upon it, his task is not to escape from it but to use it perfectly. Similarly, our incarnate flesh is the medium God has given us for working out our salvation. The doctrine of the resurrection protects the Christian doctrine of the body from corruption by both "spiritualizers" and "materializers", by teaching that because the body is real it can be redeemed, and because it is raised from the dead, its reality has eternal meaning.

The doctrine of bodily resurrection does not have much to say about life after death. The stories in the Gospels indicate in passing a few ideas about it, only one of which has particular importance here: that Jesus was raised an embodied person, not a disembodied spirit. This concept does need discussion, however, because of what it implies for the Christian doctrines of man and of history.

The simplest way of tracing its implications is by defining the three most popular theories of what happens to persons after their death. First, it is asserted that death is the complete end of the person as such. He may be remembered for a few years. His actions will continue indefinitely to influence other events. But the person himself is annihilated. Second, it is proposed that some part of the person continues to exist in some other life and some other form. The body disintegrates, but the "real" person — his soul or spirit or essence — persists, leaving behind the now worthless fleshly shell. The "spirit" or whatever is thus freed from the restrictions of matter and from its bondage to the past. This is the concept of immortality, which has consistently been repudiated in traditional Christianity, although the words "immortality" and "resurrection" have sometimes been used interchangeably. The third theory, which is the Christian one, insists that the entire person dies in all his aspects and functions, and that the entire person is raised from the dead.

Immortality affirms the death of the body only. It denies complete death, and in so doing turns the whole business to little account. It implies, in defiance of nearly all human intuition, that death is an illusion and that our sense of outrage when we confront our own or another's death can be ex-

153

plained away. By refusing to admit that our horror of death reflects the reality, by refusing to admit that death really is death, it forbids us hope. Where there is no death, neither is there the conquest of death.

Of course, if death is not real, there is no need for a conquest of death. But Christianity will have no part in the attempt to palter with death. It says that man is right to fear its ravages. Jesus himself was horrified at its approach, and dying, he felt himself abandoned by God. The Christian doctrine of the resurrection palliates nothing of death's enormity or of man's repugnance. It justifies his terror. It vindicates his grief. Then beside the reality of our terror and grief, it sets the reality of a new life in which the past is redeemed and restored.

Immortality predicates a continuation, meaning precisely an extension of this life that differs from what we now have principally, if not solely, in the absence of a confining body. Christian resurrection, however, means a new life in which the old is included and fulfilled. That which was wholly lost in death is wholly restored, and when it returns it is changed. The sharp division contains the promise of a redemption that encompasses the person whose body is the incarnation of his self. Where immortality promises a final discarnation, resurrection promises the renewal of incarnation.

According to the records of Jesus' resurrection, he was raised an embodied person whose present reality contained his whole history. He remembered it and he carried its marks in his body. His wounds were healed; what remained were scars. But the unequivocal body and the unequivocal history of the man participated in the resurrected life. The flesh was not left behind. The past was not effaced. He had totally died, and he was healed and raised from the dead in his totality.

It is the mark of ignorance or flippancy to tie up discussion of the resurrection with questions about the composition of Jesus' resurrected body, or anyone else's. We have no way of answering those questions, and it would not need to be mentioned at all except that it has been a prime ground for irrelevant argument. Indeed his body was changed, but in this life our bodies also change. Their atoms, molecules, cells alter from instant to instant. It is the body's form, its configuration, and not its physical or chemical constituents, that gives it identity, continuity, and materiality. Its organization persists in such a way that a mother can see her small child in the man he has become, and occasionally we can see in the faces of the young what they will look like when they are old. Since we can recognize a friend after twenty years of separation, in spite of the complete change in his physical components, we need not be seriously deterred by the thought of a resurrected body which would manifest only another change in composition that leaves its configuration unimpaired.

Because immortality is immeasurably the easier doctrine to comprehend, it is not surprising that so many people believe it to be Christian. They do not want death to be death, as Christianity says that it is. Yet in the unutterable bleakness when the beloved has died, the words "He is not really dead," are an insult to our minds and hearts. Then only the straitened, heartbreaking Christian doctrine can meet our knowledge and our need.

The essence of Christianity lies in the phrases "the forgiveness of sins and the resurrection of the body", taken together. The faith and the community are God-centered, not man-centered. They do not rest upon a system of ethics, a set of historical events, membership in a church, administration or reception of sacraments, affirmation of a creed or a theology, acts of worship, or any form of "religious experience". These are means for becoming Christian or concomitants of being Christian. What is absolutely central is *the act of God in Christ by which he transforms evil into good* — in technical theological terms, God's redemptive act. And he is Lord of the past and future as well as the present, of matter as well as mind and heart and spirit, of nature as well as history. The acceptance of forgiveness opens to us the way to the life of God. In the forgiveness of sins, redemption becomes incarnate. In resurrection, forgiveness has eternal life.

Chapter 21

AND THE LIFE EVERLASTING

EVERLASTING LIFE IS COMMONLY TAKEN TO MEAN ANOTHER STATE of existence following this one. Less commonly, it is interpreted as meaning that this life of time, nature, and history will go on forever: it becomes one of the ways of asserting immortality. But there is another possibility that avoids the excessive other-worldliness of the one and the excessive this-worldliness of the other: that these words refer not to a succession of lives but to a quality of life that is timeless, and therefore available here and now. Specifically, we are now, at this instant, with the everlasting God or against him, welcoming or resisting him, knowing his presence as a heaven of flaming love or a hell of tormenting fire. "This is eternal life, that they know thee the only true God, and Jesus Christ whom thou hast sent." Here and now we are living in him or dying to him, enjoying eternal life or suffering eternal death.

This is the Creed's decisive statement on meaning: that it does not lie in any temporal event, future or present or past, but in the God who is outside the created world of nature and history, yet active within it, and we can discover our meaning if we submit ourselves to him. Then and then only we become so deeply interrelated with the source of our existence that we can know who and what and where we are, and what the universe is all about. Remaining within nature and history, we attain a vantage point from which we can see them in perspective.

This has nothing whatever to do with foretelling the future, which purports to be a matter of seeing along time rather than through it. Instead, it is concerned with discovering relationships, with viewing things in proportion, with becoming aware of the co-inherent order of existence and discerning our place in it. That order has its source in God. It is worked out in the temporal sequences of the creation which, being derived from and dependent upon God, partakes in its own manner of his everlastingness. Being in him, it has eternal significance and eternal life.

The Christian faith looks toward an end that is at once an event in time and a timeless state of being. We open our hearts and minds and hands to our neighbor, and as we become deeply involved in his life, the glory of the eternal God reaches us through him. Conversely, our intuitions of eternity send us into the immediate world, to show its glory there. We cannot make ourselves accessible to one without becoming aware of the other and loving it. We can, however, close ourselves to both. If we shut our minds firmly against the authenticity of all relationships except immediate historical and natural ones, we shall participate only in the limited meanings that history and nature provide. If we go too far in such denials, we shall have at the end of our history only the living death where there is no giving and receiving, no tie of memory or anticipation, but only our self-chosen exile from everything other than our unfathomably solitary selves. Because to have life is to be in relationships of exchange. To have eternal life is to be in exchange with the eternal God.

Chapter 22

AMEN

"AMEN" BRINGS US BACK, FULL CIRCLE, TO THE BEGINNING. "SO BE it — so may it be in us" we say to the Apostles' Creed, not phrase by phrase but seeing the pattern as a whole.

The most notable characteristic of the Creed is its concern with the nature of the world we live in. Only the first three words allow us to turn our attention directly inward. In them we abandon the circumspect detachments and sophistical introversions that would restrain us from participating wholly in the wholeness of living. In them we confess our involvement with all that exists. Now we no longer hold ourselves aloof. We are committing ourselves to living in a particular way, and surveying the world from a particular position. We believe in. We have faith.

We see about us a world that we did not create and cannot entirely control. Sometimes we are lost and afraid in it. Sometimes we are at home and joyous and assured. Always we are impelled by that deepest of human needs, the compulsion to find meaning in what we do and are. Without meaning, our highest ecstasies are poisoned, our agonies break us into shreds, and a pinprick devastates us. With meaning, we may sometimes be horrified or afraid or unhappy, but we are at home in the world, and beneath the storms we have access to the passionate, glorious peace that passes all human understanding.

We who are Christian affirm the presence of meaning in all life, a meaning which includes the ends of the world and the extremes of human experience. We declare that it inheres in God. We do not claim that we know the complete meaning of all things. We do claim that in God there is one. This is an act of faith. Neither its truth nor its falsity can be indisputably

158

proved by any process of reasoning or experimentation, nor infallibly communicated to the unbelieving or the despairing.

We believe that the created world is derived from and dependent upon God, and functions according to at least three basic principles. First, only God is God. Second, all things exist by virtue of their relationships with God, and through him by their relationships with one another. Third, all life, from the single-celled to the divine, is contingent upon exchange: giving and receiving, taking in and sending forth. These principles provide the great overriding structure which supports every form and level of being, and unifies the entire wealth of existence. To the degree that our lives are consistent with this pattern, we have abundant life and our lives have meaning. If we rebel against any of its elements, we die.

This, however, is a minimum, and Christianity is not a minimal religion. It goes on to declare that God is good and that the facts of relationship and exchange are good. But we have developed an antagonism to the good and to God. While we do not know when or under what circumstances this condition originated, all our knowledge of mankind confirms the Christian testimony that we are divided beings, at once loving the good and hating it, desiring to subject ourselves to God and to make ourselves gods.

It is conceivable that God might cast us off because of our rebellion, but he does not. Instead, he does everything he can to restore us, short of forcing us against our wills. In particular, he gives his life for us, and he gives us the gift of the Holy Spirit to encourage and direct us toward him. He waits for us with forgiveness and the promise of redemption. Jesus the Christ introduced into nature and history the full vitality of forgiving and redeeming love. He showed us what God does for us, and what we can do. He broke for us the strangling web of our antagonism.

We can follow him out of that tangle, but we are not compelled to. We can have his life or our own death, as we choose. No one can avoid that decision: we follow God's will or some other will. We cannot serve two masters without suffering the disintegrity that leads to death. Because we are finite, we do

159

not and cannot know absolutely, ultimately, and irrefutably that the choice for God in Christ Jesus is the best, or even the good, *all* things considered. Nonetheless, we must take our stand.

Throughout Christian history, the worst threats to the Christian faith have come not from ignorance or misinterpretation or deliberate falsification, but from superficiality, and especially the idolatry that arises when one of our functions or responsibilities is emphasized at the expense of the others. There are the aesthetes who seek from the faith mainly an emotional glow of security or uplift. There are the activists to whom Christianity means primarily or only certain forms of behavior. There are the dogmatists who set up correct knowledge as their standard, ignoring the needs of the heart and the calls for action. But Christianity is not merely or even essentially aesthetic, activist, or dogmatic. It is personal, and to neglect or exaggerate any of these functions is to make the faith to some degree impersonal.

If the aesthete were to apply his intellect to his faith, and set himself to discipline his will, he would also have to discipline his emotional self-indulgence, but he would discover in himself more subtle and penetrating responses. The activist who determined to explore theology and the life of devotion would find his energies redirected and concentrated. He would scurry less and get more work done. A dogmatist who sought to increase the depth and breadth of his faith would have to sacrifice some of the meticulous purity of his concepts and language, but he would gain immeasurably in richness and power of concern. Perfect balance of functions may not be possible or even desirable, and a person or group or congregation may take an extreme position as a way of counterbalancing another extreme in the society around it. But gross imbalance is clearly possible and emphatically not desirable. At the least, what one cannot do for himself, he can love and adore in another. Christians and Christian organizations which profess or practise superficial forms of Christianity will attract only the shallow, and will destroy in themselves and for others the hope that in Jesus the Christ can be found a life that is not superficial

but that meets the complete range of man's needs and the height
of his vision.

A NOTE ON SOURCES

Readers who are familiar with the writings of Charles Williams, C. S. Lewis, G. K. Chesterton, and Charles Morgan will recognize how profoundly and in how many ways I am indebted to their work. Less obviously, I owe almost as much to Jules Laurence Moreau's *Language and Religious Language*, John V. Taylor's *The Primal Vision*, and John Macmurray's Gifford Lectures, *The Self As Agent* and *Persons in Relation*.

I am deeply grateful both to the laymen who read this book in its early drafts and whose encouragement prevented me from abandoning it at times when I became discouraged, and to the three critics of the final draft whose penetration, wisdom, and learning rectified many defects of omission and commission: the Reverend Clifford W. Atkinson, Betsy Ward Pitha, and my husband, Emerson W. Shideler. They are not, however, responsible for errors or lacunae in the content of the book, or awkwardness in its structure or style.

It is more than twenty-five years since I studied under Dr. Robert B. MacLeod. He will probably be astonished — possibly he will be appalled — at the direction I have taken since then, but nothing I have thought or written during those years is untouched by his influence. The dedication is my acknowledgement that I owe him far more than I can identify, much less repay.

NOTES

Epigraph, title page: Charles Williams, "Dr. Joad and Sin". *Time and Tide*, Vol. 24, No. 11, March 13, 1943, p. 212.

1. Jules Laurence Moreau, *Language and Religious Language*. Philadelphia: The Westminster Press, 1960, p. 45.
2. Charles Williams, *Rochester*. London: Arthur Barker, Ltd., 1935, p. 239.
3. See John Macmurray, *The Self As Agent* and *Persons in Relation*, London: Faber and Faber, Limited, 1957 and 1961.
4. Charles Williams, "Transition and Decision". *Time and Tide*, Vol. 21, No. 10, March 9, 1940, p. 255.
5. Charles Morgan, *Sparkenbroke*. London: Macmillan and Co., Ltd., 1936, Book II, Chapter ii.
6. Charles Williams, "The Death of Good Fortune". *Collected Plays*. London: Oxford University Press, 1963, p. 194.

7. T. S. Eliot, "The Dry Salvages". *Four Quartets*. London: Faber and Faber, Limited, 1943, line 215.

8. George Macdonald, "The Consuming Fire". *Unspoken Sermons,* Series I, London: Alexander Strahan, 1867, p. 37.

9. Gregory Vlastos, *The Religious Way*. New York: The Woman's Press, 1934, p. 9.

10. G. W. Target, *We, the Crucifiers*. London: Hodder and Stoughton, Ltd., 1964, pp. 138-139, 141.

11. Dorothy L. Sayers, *The Man Born to Be King*. New York: Harper and Brothers, 1943, p. 5.

12. C. S. Lewis, *The Discarded Image*. Cambridge: The University Press, 1964, p. 119.

13. Evelyn Underhill, *The Letters of Evelyn Underhill*. London: Longmans, Green and Co., 1943, p. 140.

14. C. S. Lewis, *An Experiment in Criticism*. Cambridge: The University Press, 1961, p. 128.

15. Jeremy Taylor, *Life of Christ*. In *Works,* edited by Heber, 1847, Vol. II, Part 1, Sec. 5, para. 27.

16. Charles Morgan, *The River Line: A Play*. London: Macmillan and Co., Ltd., 1952, Act III, Scene 2.

17. Charles Williams, "The Cross". *The Image of the City and Other Essays,* edited by Anne Ridler. London: Oxford University Press, 1958, p. 137.

18. See Charles Williams, *The Descent of the Dove*. Grand Rapids: Wm. B. Eerdmans Publishing Co., 1939, p. 62.

19. C. S. Lewis, "Williams and the Arthuriad". *Arthurian Torso*. London: Oxford University Press, 1948, p. 142.

20. The *Quicunque vult:* the formula known as the Athanasian Creed.

INDEX

Action, 31-32, 34, 37
Agnosticism, 32
Alienation, 24, 54, 67, 83, 103, 114
Anthropomorphism, 60
Art, 62-63, 69, 74, 83, 130, 152-153
Ascension, 121-123
Athanasian Creed, 19, 110, 147
Authority, 26-27, 28-30, 40, 101-102,
    126-128

Beauty, 33
Belief, types of, 25-35, 46-47, 100,
    140-141, 152 (see also Faith)
Bible, 10, 71-72, 95, 99-100, 150
Body, 9-10, 65, 66-67, 84, 94, 105-
    106, 122-123, 152-155
Bonhoeffer, Dietrich, 45
Both-and propositions, 31

Causality, 38
Certainty, 25-35, 39, 50
Choice, among beliefs, 47-49, 100,
    113-115, 122, 142-143, 159-160;
    necessity for, 31-32, 51-52, 76-77
Christianity, definitions of, 12-18, 46,
    49, 57, 68-69, 140-147, 155, 160
Christians, isolated, 144-145
Church, doctrine of, 11, 18, 24,
    140-147
Churches, local congregations, 12,
    144-147
Coherence, 32-33, 39
Co-inherence, see Exchange
Commitment, see Choice
Communion of saints, 140-143
Confession, 131
Contemplative tradition, 36
Conversion, 119, 151
Courage, 37-38, 40-41
Covenanted gifts, 111
Creation, 32-33, 67, 71-72, 105-106,
    127, 136-137
Creaturehood, 126-127
Creeds, 17-24, 57, 110, 136-137
Criminal negligence, 97, 108
Crucifixion, 107-108, 114
Cynicism, 38

Damnation, 113-115
Dante, 38, 102-103, 114
Death, 77, 109-110, 119-120, 153-155
Death-of-God theology, 45
Decision, 28, 41, 47-49 (see also
    Choice, Responsibility)
Democracy, 126-127
Dependence, 115, 150, 159
Derivation, 47, 57-60, 104-105, 111,
    137, 146, 159
Despair, 79, 97, 103
Detachment, 23-24, 89, 158
Diversity, 64-66, 127
Docetism, 99, 121
Dogmatism, 13, 38, 125, 160

Eclecticism, 68
Either-or propositions, 31-32, 79
Elegance, 33, 39
Eliot, T. S., 84
Emotion, 27, 49, 58-59, 79, 83, 87-89
Encounter of God and man, 28, 46,
    48-50, 99-102, 112, 121-122, 131-
    132
Equality, 126-128, 142, 147
Eschatology, 129-132, 156-157
Eternity, 82, 129, 156-157
Ethics, 9, 34, 64, 76-77, 110
Evil, 64, 67, 75-80, 83, 118 (see also
    Sin)
Evolution, 28, 30, 32-33, 71-74, 117
Exchange, principle of, 64-70, 77-79,
    84-85, 115, 122, 136-137, 151, 157-
    159; love as, 88-89, 136-137;
    natural, 75, 77, 102, 111, 142-143
    150-151
Existentialism, 103

Faith, 13, 36-41, 59, 61, 110-111, 158
    (see also Belief)
Fatherhood, 57-61
Father-images, 60-61
Fear, 37-38
Figures of speech, 113, 124-126
Fire-walking, 117
Flesh, see Body
Forgiveness, 108, 148-152, 155

165

Freedom, 51-52, 67, 69, 72, 77-79, 109, 113, 130, 138, 142

Gnosticism, 66-67, 105
God, 10-14, 29, 37, 45-55, 74-80, 86-87 (see also Holy Spirit, Jesus, Omnipotence, Trinity)
Good, 64, 75-80, 86-87, 96, 111, 159
Greek thought, 15, 66
Guilt, 96, 113, 130

Heaven, 67, 81-84, 113-115
Hebrew thought, 15, 70, 71-72, 136
Hell, 113-115
Heresy, 66-67, 99, 121, 153, 160
Hierarchy, principle of, 126-128, 142, 147
History, 16, 19, 70, 84, 106, 116-120, 148, 152-157
Holiness, 68-69, 96, 102, 106, 123, 143
Holy Spirit, 101, 105, 135-139, 146-147, 151, 159
Hope, 79, 98, 103, 130, 154
Humanism, 99
Hume, David, 38
Humility, 39, 53, 101, 138

Idolatry, 96, 160
Ignorance, 94, 96-97
Imagery, 60-61, 81-82, 113, 124-125, 137
Immortality, 153-156
Incarnation, 84, 104-106, 109, 123, 145 (see also Body, Church, Jesus, Resurrection)
Inclusiveness, 33, 39
Individuality, 24, 67, 68, 94
Initiative, 101, 139, 143
Integrity, 13-14, 54-55, 62, 67, 69-70, 111, 135, 148, 151-152
Intolerance, 53-54
Isaiah, 139

Jesus, 67, 98-101, 104-106, 121-122, 129, 146, 154, 159 (see also Crucifixion, Death, Resurrection, Trinity, Virgin Birth); teachings of, 30, 87, 110-112
Judas Iscariot, 130
Judgement, 129-132, 135
Justice, 129-131

Knowledge, 25-39, 51, 76-77, 101, 141 (see also Reason)

Laity, 10-14
Language, 9, 13-14, 18-19, 56, 81-82, 99, 102, 124-125, 135
Language analysis, 45-46, 74
Leap of faith, 100-101
Lewis, C. S., 14, 117, 124-125, 142
Love, 10, 30, 64, 68, 86-89, 115, 136-138
Loyalty, 141, 147
Luther, Martin, 27

Macdonald, George, 97
Man, 62-63, 67, 73, 141-142, 146; as finite, 28-30, 33, 35, 51-54, 124, 159-160; Christian doctrine of, 66-67, 93-103, 122-123, 131; "modern", 13-14, 45, 81-83
Materialism, 51, 121
Matter, 9-10, 105-106, 121 (see also Body)
Meaning, 62-63, 71, 73-75, 153, 156-157, 158
Meaninglessness, 73-74, 94
Milton, John, 114
Miracles, 51
Moreau, Jules Laurence, 17
Morgan, Charles, 14, 66, 129
Mysticism, 36, 48-49, 74

Natural law, 69-70, 104-106
Nature, 62-70, 105-106, 116-120, 129-130, 148, 152-155, 156-157
Necessity, 68-69, 89, 142, 146
Nicene Creed, 19, 110, 136-137
Non-Christian religions, 33, 52-53, 60, 66-68, 86, 94, 103, 111

Obedience, 27, 75, 106, 126-128
Omnipotence, 71, 75-80, 98, 118, 137-138
Otherness, 48-50, 54, 58, 84-85

Pantheism, 123
Person, 46-48, 54, 63-65, 66-70, 75, 131-132, 152-155
Philosophy, 10, 38, 45-46
Preference, 39, 54

Presuppositions, 26-29, 30-35, 37, 51, 63
Pride, 38-39
Probability, 30, 72-73
Proof, 25-29, 34-35, 50-52, 73, 158-160
Purposiveness, 63

Reality, 9-10, 82, 96, 110, 113
Reason, 26-30, 39-40, 46, 54 (see also Knowledge, Man as finite, Proof)
Redemption, 77, 80, 98-99, 102-103, 114, 118-120, 151-152, 154-155 (see also Salvation)
Religious experience, 49-50 (see also Emotion, Mysticism)
Repentance, 149, 151-152
Resistance and support, 27, 50, 58-59
Responsibility, 11-12, 23-24, 36, 78, 103, 109, 114, 129-130, 138
Resurrection, 67, 109-110, 116-120, 152-155
Revelation, 27-28, 69

Sacramental world view, 123, 143
Sacraments, 123, 131, 143, 144
Saint Paul, 36, 67, 102
Saints, 140
Salvation, 68, 98-99, 106, 111, 148, 152-153
Sartre, Jean-Paul, 45
Sayers, Dorothy L., 108-109
Science, 14, 39, 50-51, 69, 73-74, 82-83, 116-118 (see also Evolution, Knowledge, Proof)
Security, 50
Self-knowledge, 63, 131-132, 152

Sense experience, 25-26, 28, 30, 117
Sin, 94-99, 108-109, 118, 130-131, 145, 148-152, 159; original sin, 96-97
Skepticism, 13, 29-30, 37-40, 51
Social justice, 76, 83, 94
Spirit, 66-67, 84, 94, 138
Supernaturalism, 49, 62, 81-82

Target, G. W., 107-108
Taylor, Jeremy, 125
Theology, 9-15, 34, 40, 110-112, 140
Thomas the Doubter, 27
Time, 156-157 (see also Eternity, History)
Tolerance, 53-54
Transcendence, 49, 81-85
Trinity, 122, 126-128, 135-139 (see also God, Holy Spirit, Jesus)
Truth, 9, 34-35, 52-53

Underhill, Evelyn, 121

Values, 67, 86, 105-106, 124-125
Virgin Mary, 105-106
Vlastos, Gregory, 100

Will, 69, 87-89, 95-96
Williams, Charles, 14, 49, 59, 64, 79, 130, 135
Wisdom, 17, 132
Wish-fulfilment, 50
Wonder, 50, 71-73
Work, 142-143
World views, 39-40, 53, 62-63, 81, 110-112, 119-120, 123, 143, 158-159 (see also Meaning)
Worship, 13, 50, 59, 84